Michael T. Winstanley SDB

Echoes for the Soul

Don Bosco Publications

Don Bosco Publications
Thornleigh House, Sharples Park, Bolton BL1 6PQ
United Kingdom

ISBN 978-1-909080-94-2

Printed in Malta by Melita Press

FSC www.fsc.org MIX Paper from responsible sources FSC® C004116

Preface

Some months ago, whilst on retreat with my religious community, I heard a talk about the use of social media for educational and evangelising purposes. The thought occurred to me that it was time I moved out of my comfort zone and attempted something new. I suggested to Fr Bob Gardner and Ms Sarah Seddon at Don Bosco Publications that each weekday I might post a photo of mine with a relevant reflection. They accepted the idea and, using the title Echoes for the Soul, posted these in Salesian Link on Facebook. The response has been very positive, and now, with creativity and great skill, they have transformed a selection of photos and reflections into an attractive book. For this, I am deeply appreciative and excited.

For many years, I have enjoyed photography. It is a challenging and satisfying hobby and, with digital technology, has endless possibilities. My camera enables me to capture a moment in time, a place, a scene, an experience, which has meant something to me. These images, now on file in the computer, can easily be revisited, and the special moments experienced anew. The photos can also be shared with others in the hope that they, too, will find inspiration and pleasure in them. A picture can evoke a wide spectrum of emotional responses. The reflections in the book are an expression of my thoughts and feelings on a particular morning at the desk, highlighting one aspect which has touched me in a distinctive way. For the reader, I hope that the photos and reflections of this book can be a springboard for further pondering, perhaps a little daily oasis, and a source of wonder and enjoyment within the mystery of God's world and love.

Thornleigh House, Bolton.
December 15, 2022.

Copyright Acknowledgement

Contents

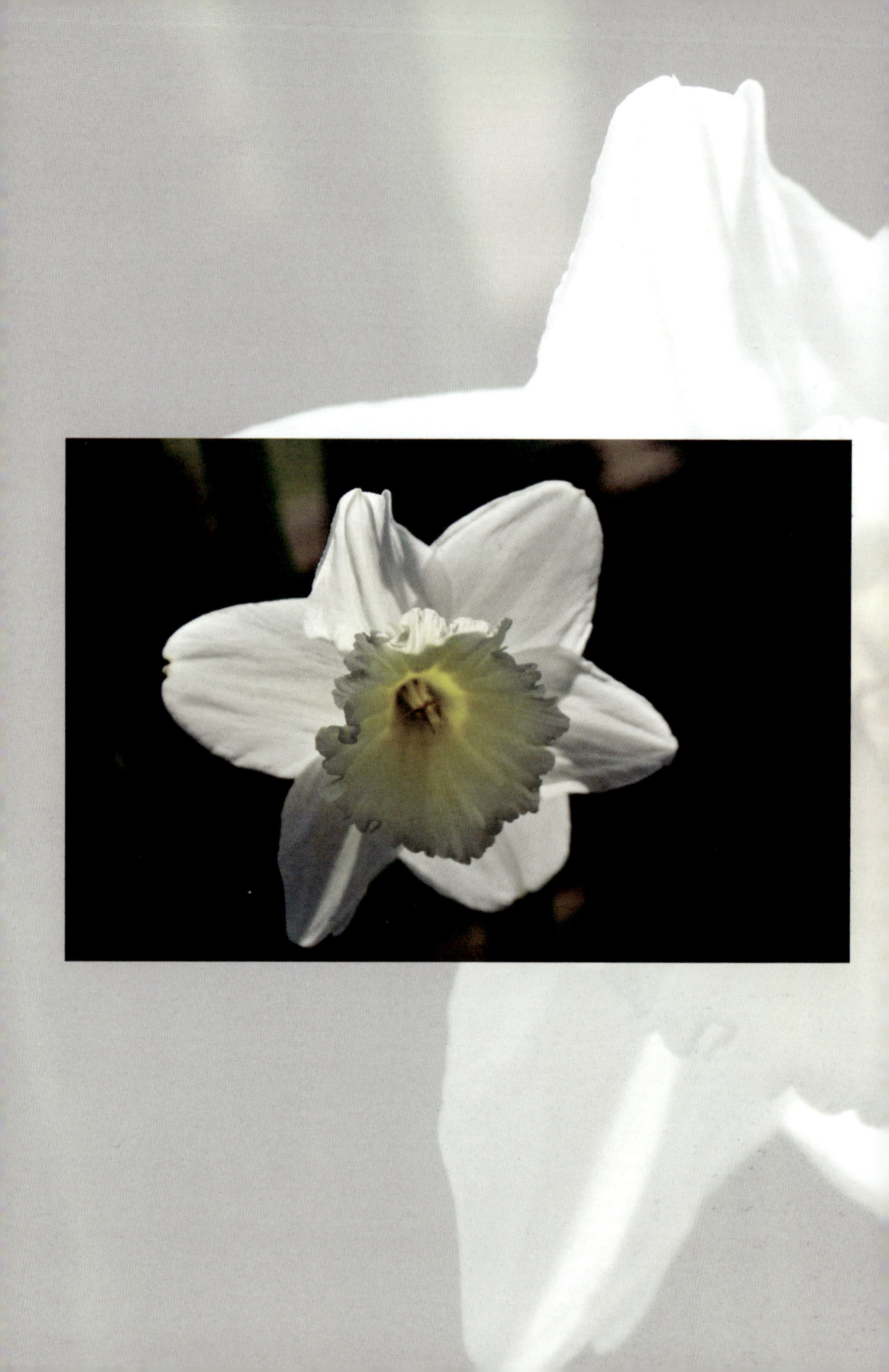

A Smile from God

I've chosen this recent photo simply because I love it. Most of our daffodils are varieties of bright yellow as they welcome the spring, dispelling the dark of winter, harbingers of hope and future. In our garden this year there were a few daffodils which caught my eye because they were white, and I couldn't resist taking a photo. I think this one is quite awesome in the beauty of its shape, texture and colour. I chose it for my electronic Easter card, since the trumpet reminded me of the empty tomb, and the central bright glow suggested the light of resurrection.

Today, let's try to be alert and open to the natural beauty around us; let's pause a little and quietly ponder in appreciation and wonder. Such flowers, such moments, have been called 'a smile from God'.

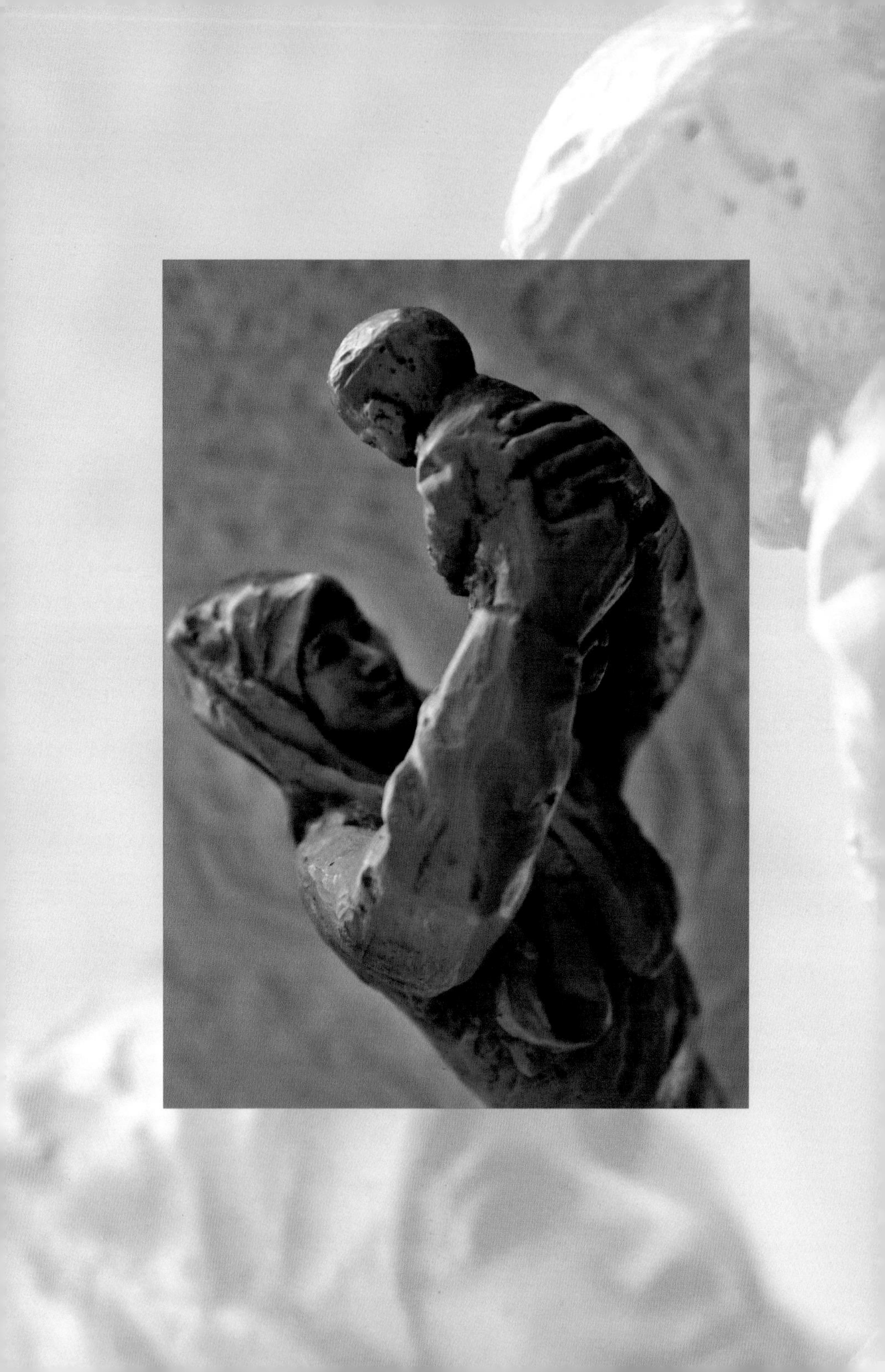

Wonderful are Your Works

There are countless pictures and statues of our Blessed Mother, many by world-famous artists and sculptors. Doubtless, we all have our favourites. This very unusual small wooden statue of Mary was given to me some years ago. It's my favourite. Mary is holding her young baby aloft, with love and excitement, joy and wonder at the new life in her hands. 'My little child.' Mary seems so human, such a natural, homely mother.

Although millions of children are born each day, I believe each is a little miracle. It's so important that we don't lose that sense of wonder at the little bundle of life a mother holds in her arms, that unbelievably complex phenomenon which is a human person, a small being with enormous potential. The psalmist puts it very beautifully: "For it was you who formed my inward parts; you knit me together in my mother's womb. I praise you, for I am fearfully and wonderfully made. Wonderful are your works." (Ps 139)

Let's today pause, and ponder the wonder of our being, rediscover the miracle that we are.

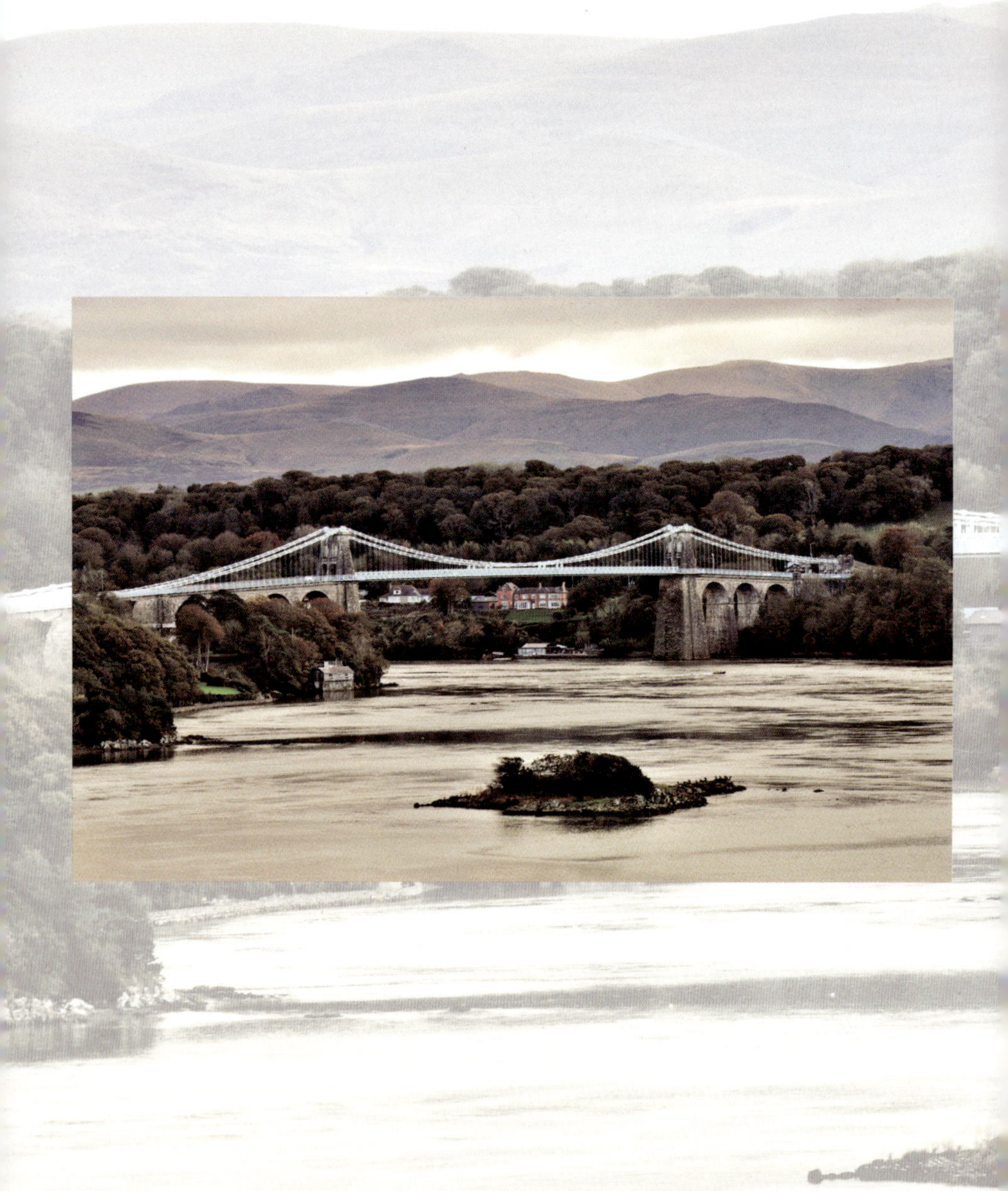

Links

For many fans of Simon and Garfunkel, their favourite number is 'Bridge over Troubled Waters', and I'm one of them, though it isn't easy to sing, given the high notes. It is a beautiful and powerful piece of music. There is something fascinating about bridges, whether they are old or modern, in our own country or elsewhere across our world. This photo, taken last November, celebrates Menai Suspension Bridge, designed by Thomas Telford, and opened in 1826. It links the Isle of Anglesey with the mainland, over the treacherous Menai Strait. It is a great piece of engineering, and also very beautiful against the backdrop of the Snowdonia mountains (Yr Wyddfa).

The keyword here is 'links'. Bridges link people and places. They facilitate communication at many levels. They unify, overcoming what separates and isolates. They remind us of something central to our following of Jesus. Jesus is the great bridge-builder, the Pontifex par excellence, the bridge between God and humanity. In his ministry he sought to bring people together, to break down barriers, to create new levels of fellowship, acceptance, reconciliation and family. As his followers, we continue his mission. Let's build a bridge or two today.

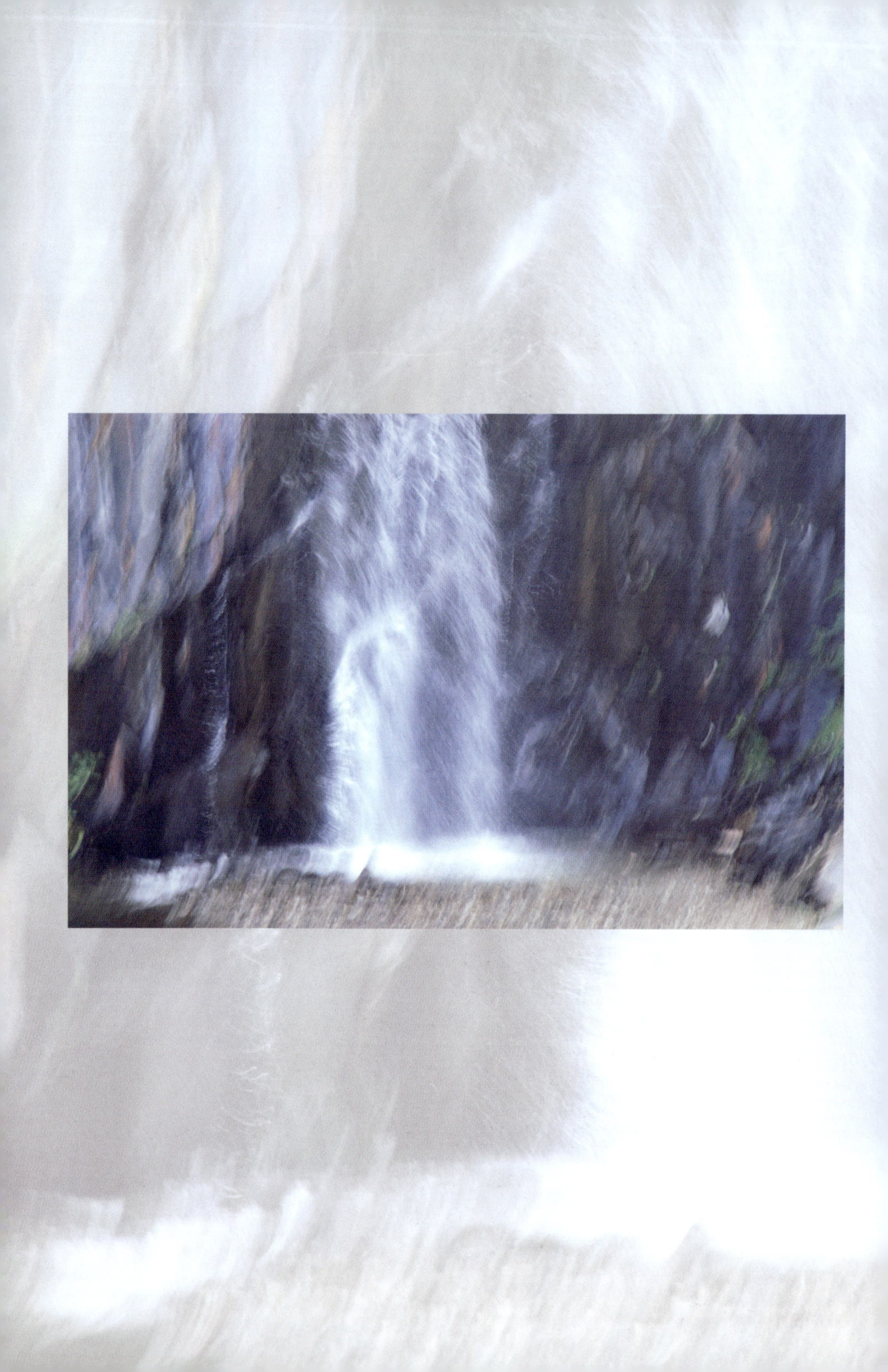

Mistakes Happen

We all make mistakes. Most of us are better at noticing the mistakes others make than at recognising and acknowledging our own. Some mistakes are quite trivial and have few repercussions; other mistakes can have serious consequences. Some mistakes can lead to positive effects; we can learn from them, and improve, and move on.

This photo, as you may have suspected, is a mistake. It was a windy day, and I wanted to get close up to this waterfall with my zoom lens, which is quite heavy, and I hadn't brought my tripod, and I failed to keep sufficiently still to take a sharp picture. I could pretend that this was an example of ICM, intentional camera movement, which is becoming an increasingly popular photographic genre, but it isn't; it is a mistake. However, the results are rather attractive, I think. It brings out very effectively the colours in the rock face, contrasting with the ethereal feel of the water. The colours would probably have been less striking on a clear, sharp image.

So today, let's try to be more willing to acknowledge our mistakes; let's not entertain denial. Let's seek to see in our mistakes the potential for change and growth. Let's not be afraid to ask Jesus' help in this, and the help of those we trust. Perhaps we can also help others to learn from their mistakes too, rather than become discouraged.

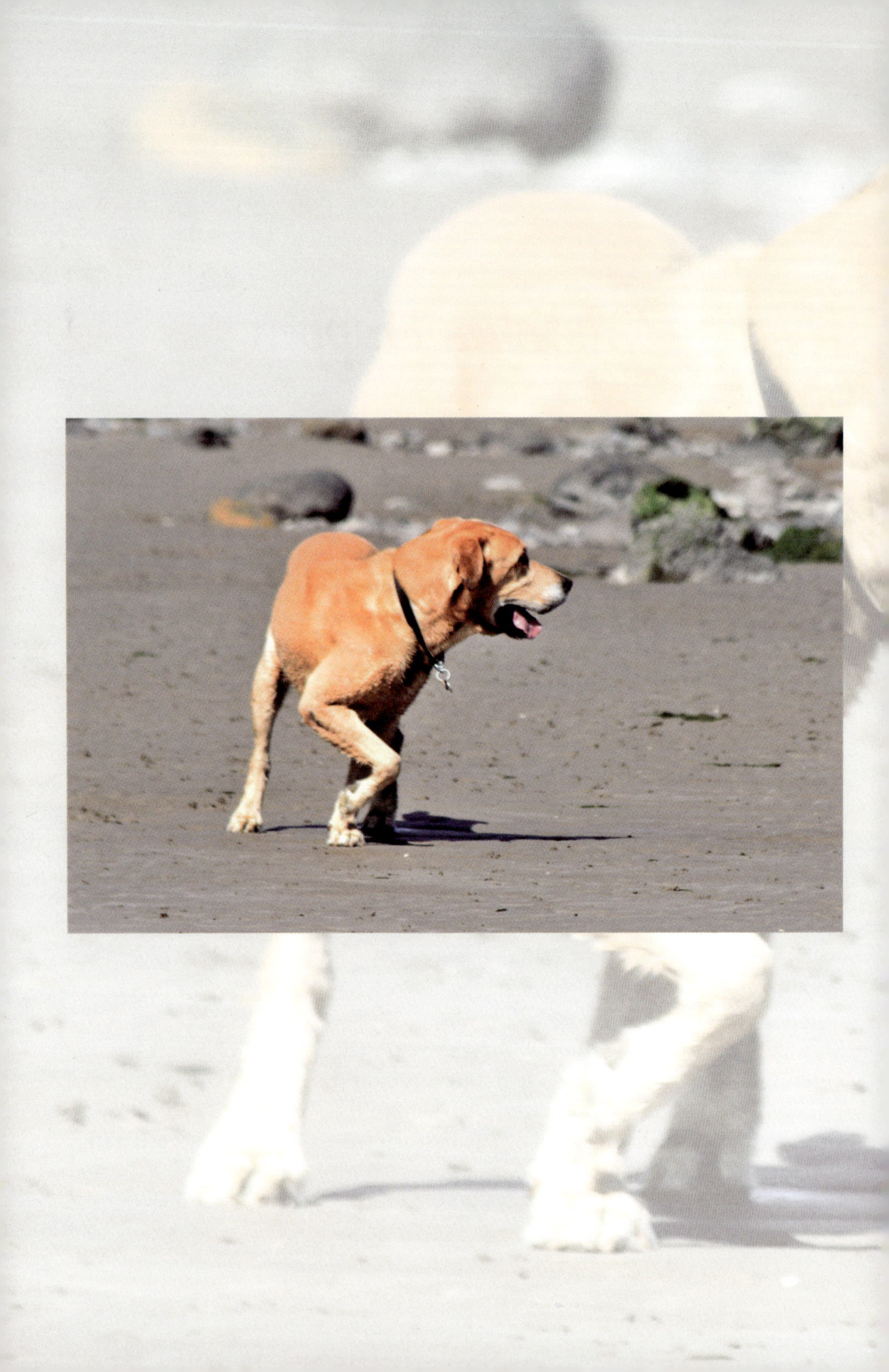

Obedience

This golden Labrador, now deceased, was called Bill, a great friend of mine. I captured this shot on the sands of Morecambe Bay where I was wandering with two other great friends, also recently deceased, Br Donald and Fr Harry. Bill is poised for action, waiting for a signal from his owner, a model of joyful obedience.

Obedience is an interesting concept with all kinds of connotations. There is that obedience which enables organisations to function, like the army or the church. There is obedience which is the result of dialogue, discussion, discernment. In religious circles we talk about obeying God's will. One of the so-called liberation theologians maintains, wisely I believe, that God's will is always that we seek to discern in any situation what love demands, and then try to respond positively and generously. What is love demanding of you today?

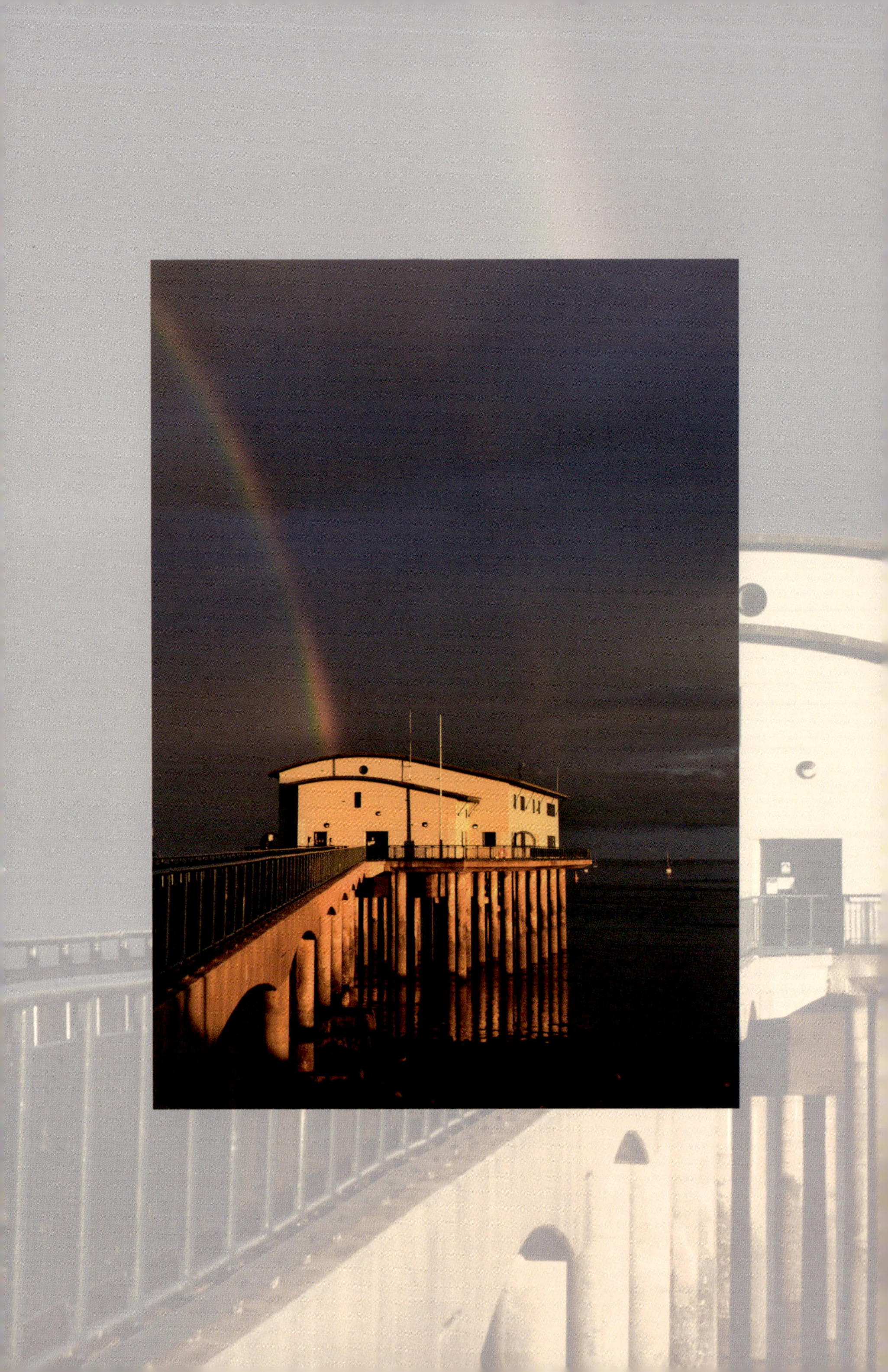

Generous Service

This is a sunset photo, though the sun was behind me! The experts often tell us to look over our shoulders when taking photos of sunsets, since the colours in the sky can be very beautiful. On this evening, they were right, and there was a rainbow present too, and reflections. The Barrow lifeboat station is situated on a small promontory known as Roa Island, which is across the strait from the island of Walney. It serves Morecambe Bay and the Irish Sea beyond. It is run by volunteers, who are summoned by phone when there is an emergency. These ordinary working people are prepared to risk their lives in coming to the rescue of sailors and ships in distress. Volunteers also join the Mountain Rescue Service in many parts of our country, well trained, ready to down tools at the call, and set off to find and help a climber or walker in difficulty, often in dangerous places and atrocious weather conditions.

Generosity takes many forms. The generosity of folk like this is steeled by courage and expertise. It also demands patience and acceptance, since often the tricky situations which have arisen are caused by thoughtlessness and foolhardiness. The sea and the mountains demand respect, reverence even. What are the qualities of your generosity today? Do you do or say things which create risks and problems for others? How far are you prepared to go to be of service to those in need? Perhaps today we could pray for those involved in these important volunteer organisations.

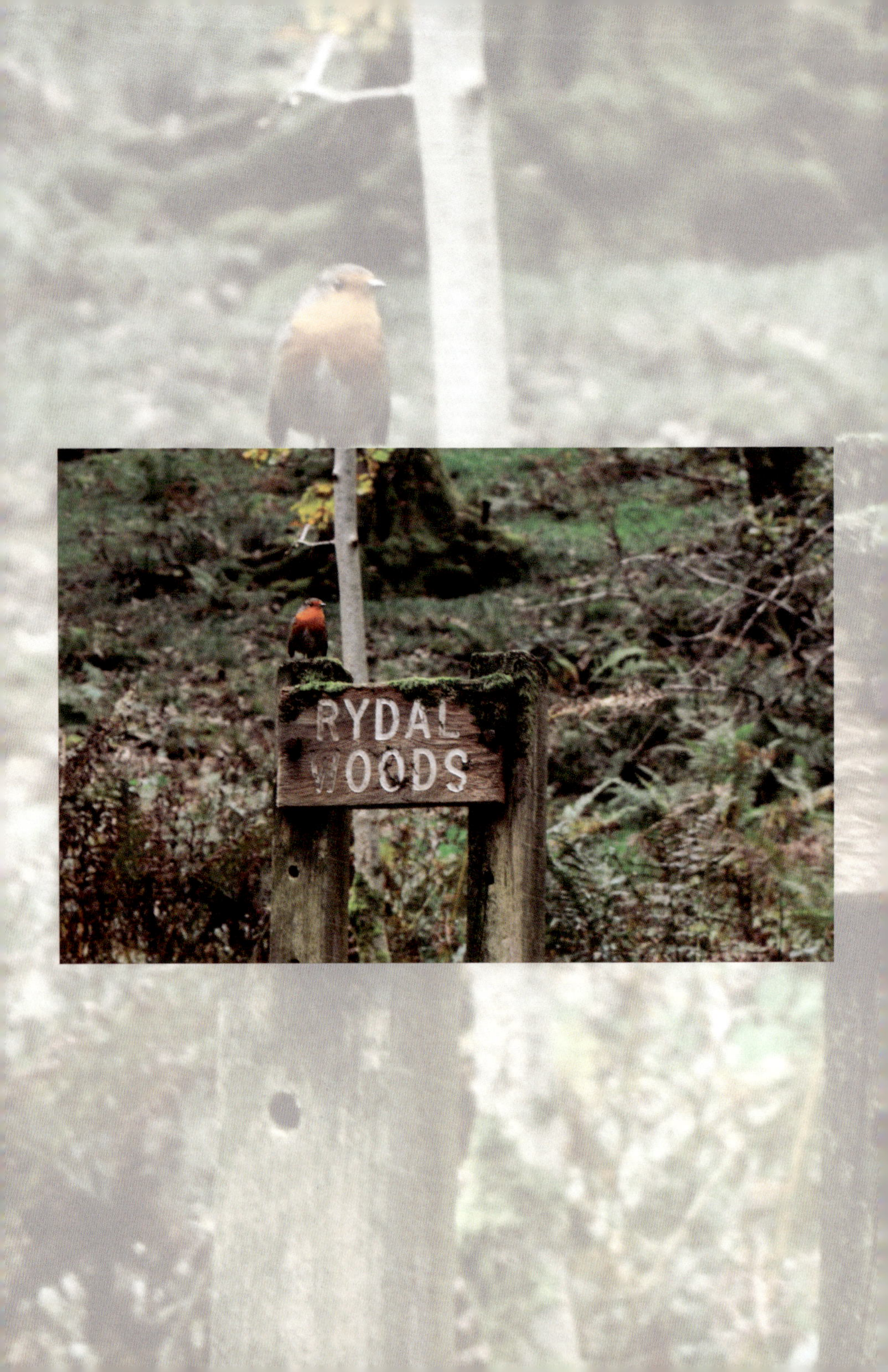
RYDAL
WOODS

A Cheerful Presence

Everyone likes a robin. They are cheeky and friendly little birds, often popping up in the garden with an air of proprietorship. I believe that they can be extremely territorial. Approaching Rydal Water one day, this little fellow perched conveniently for me, his red breast standing out against the rather dull background. I think we naturally break into a smile when we catch sight of a robin. There is something cheering about them; they brighten up the day for us.

Some human beings are like that, aren't they? Their cheerful presence can gently transform a situation, whether in the home, the school, the workplace, the bus, the shop… They lift our spirits, bringing a smile to our face. Today, let's try to be aware of these individuals, and grateful for the cheerfulness they radiate. And let's try, robin-like, to be a cheerful presence for others.

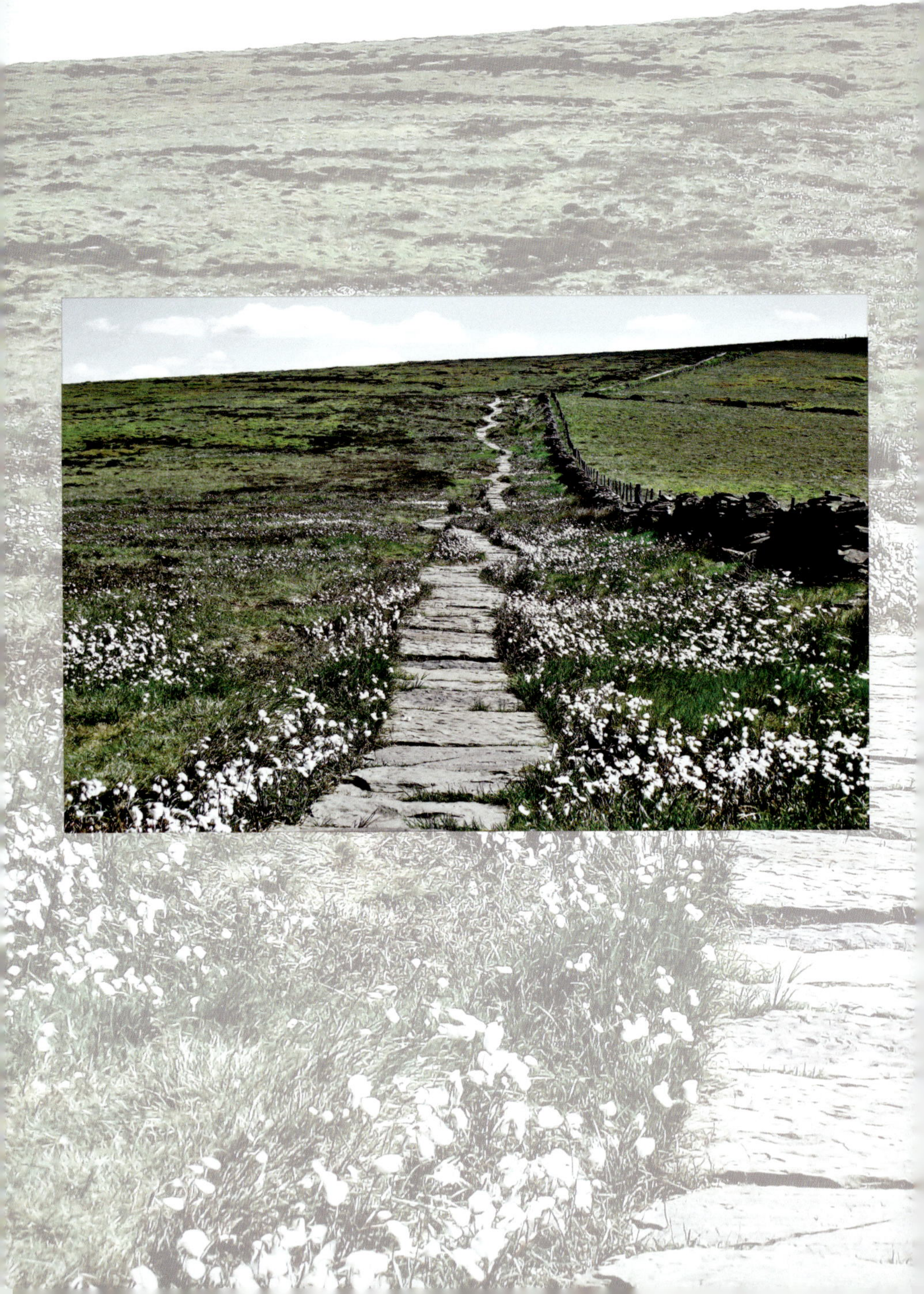

Life's Journey

For many years I lived in Savio House, our Salesian Youth Retreat Centre near Macclesfield. It is situated on the southern edge of the (Dark) Peak District, an ideal centre for walking. An interesting and demanding circular walk leaves Pym's Chair, and takes the ridge line through Cat's Tor to Shining Tor, before descending into Goyt Valley. The moorland can be boggy and forbidding, but the authorities kindly laid these flagstones to make walking easier. Sadly, the drystone walls, a relic of earlier years, are in poor condition, but the cotton grass brightens up the terrain.

Pictures like this suggest the theme of making a journey. Most journeys have clear objectives. The first objective on this journey is barely visible in the top right hand corner; it is a signpost at the summit. The pathway for me is symbolic of other journeys in life, some demanding and difficult, others less so. There are relationship journeys, health journeys, faith journeys. Most ventures, like this walk, have their ups and downs, some demand careful planning; most require patience and effort. Some can be solo attempts, others are better undertaken with others. What journeys are you involved in or projecting today? "Lord, stay with us on our journey." We are never alone.

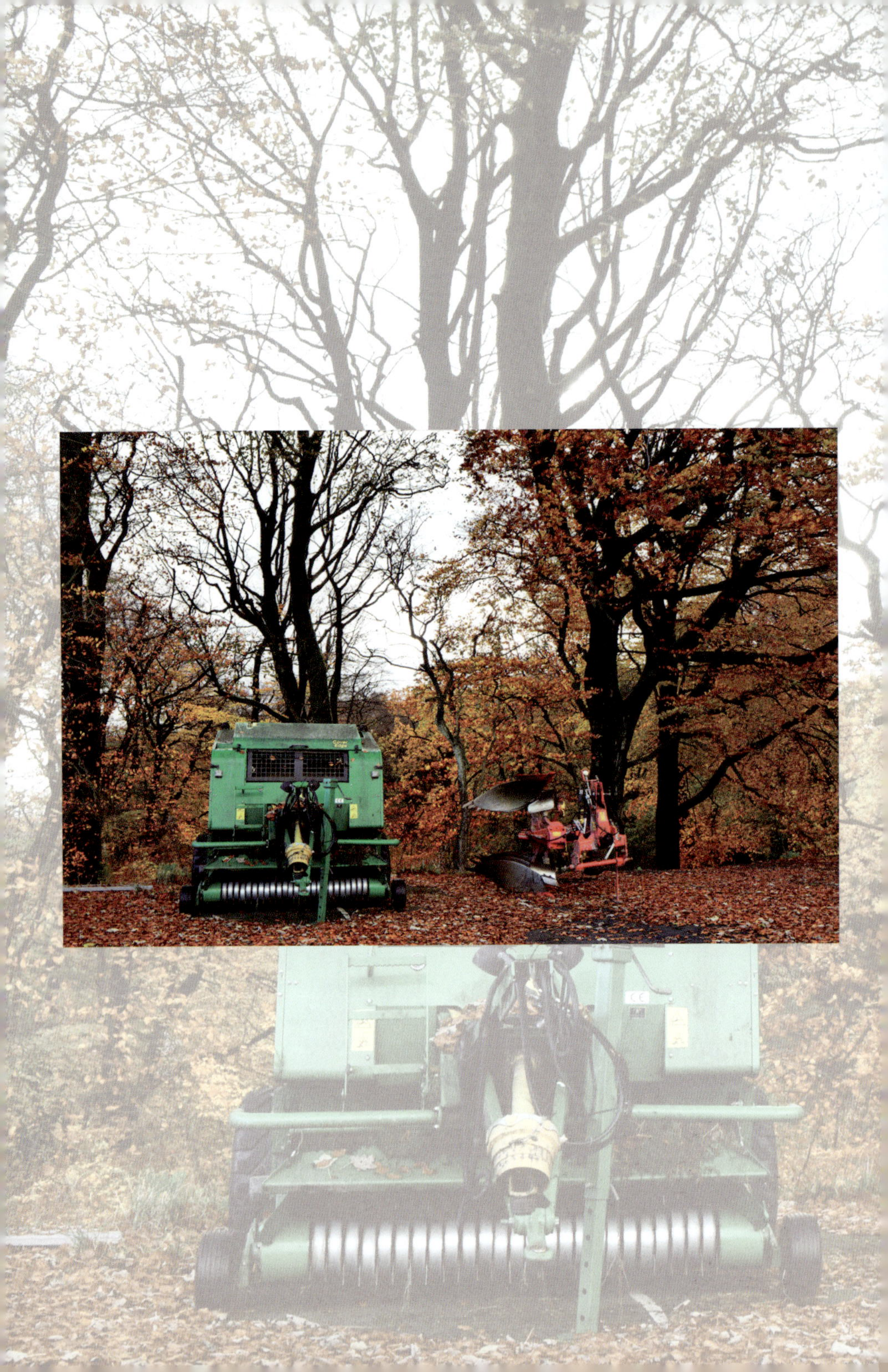

Working Together

Our community house at Thornleigh is situated on the edge of the Smithills Estate, a wide area with many paths open to the public. One major feature is the farm, an open farm usually thronged with visitors, especially children and young people. Some days there can be as many as five coaches or buses, and a hundred cars, alongside a couple of tractors and ten milkvans in the three carparks. During the COVID lockdown, the farm was quiet, the carparks empty. Wandering that way one sunny autumn day, I came across this scene. The two farm implements were parked conveniently on the edge of the vacant carpark, against a backdrop of magnificent autumn colours. I don't know the purpose of these fascinating pieces of machinery, but I felt that their shape and colour enhanced the scene.

It's wonderful when nature and human creativity are in harmony. In these days, with so much emphasis on conservation and ecological issues, we have become more aware of our need to keep it that way. Perhaps today we could think about this, notice where it is happening, and see if we can make a contribution in our locality.

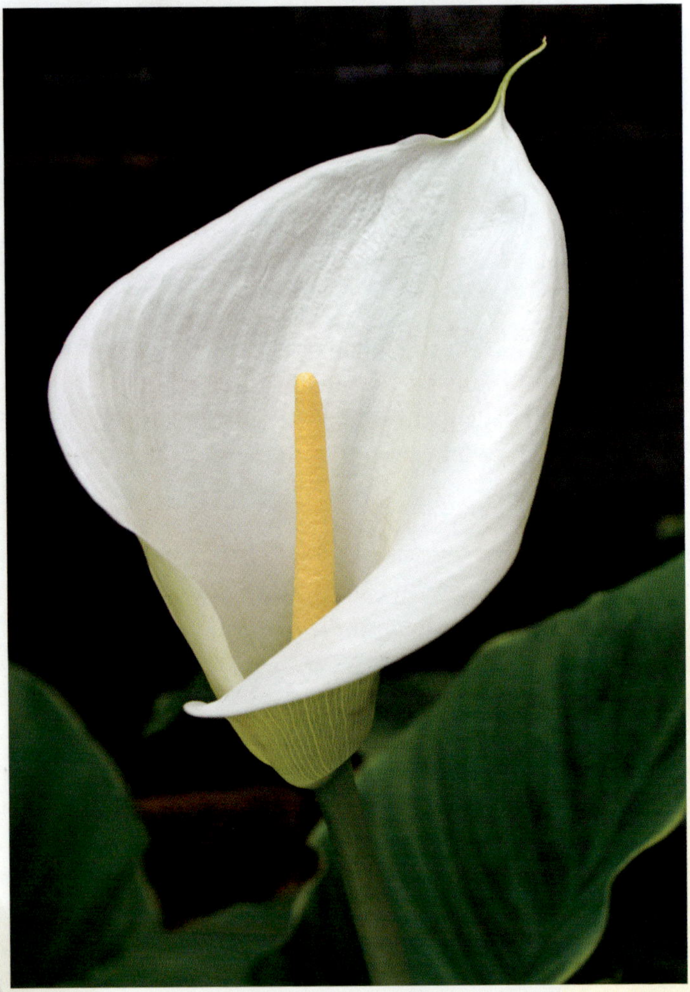

Perfection in Integrity

I think this is a perfect lily. I stumbled across it in Hinsley Hall, Leeds, the diocesan pastoral centre, where we were holding our province retreat. It stood quite near one of the house walls and could easily be missed. I find it stunning in its form, texture and hue. Apart from its beauty, it raises for me the issue of perfection.

There are people who can't abide imperfection at any level and of any kind. Given human frailty and limitations, such an attitude creates a burden for them and a problem for others. At times expectations can be wildly exaggerated, and disappointment and disapproval are inevitable. In the famous sermon on the mount, Jesus is quoted by Matthew as saying: "Be perfect as your heavenly Father is perfect." In terms of our spirituality, this incredibly high ideal is a recipe for anxiety, guilt, discouragement and a constant sense of failure, given the flaws in our makeup and living. And we are adept at noting the flaws in others, which is one way of coping with our own. But "perfect" is probably not the best translation of the Gospel passage. The word really has to do with integrity and wholeness. Since the Father is always true to Himself, Jesus is encouraging us to seek to be genuine, to be people of integrity, to be true to the unique person we are. Whether perfect or not, the lily is immensely beautiful and wonderful, just like us!

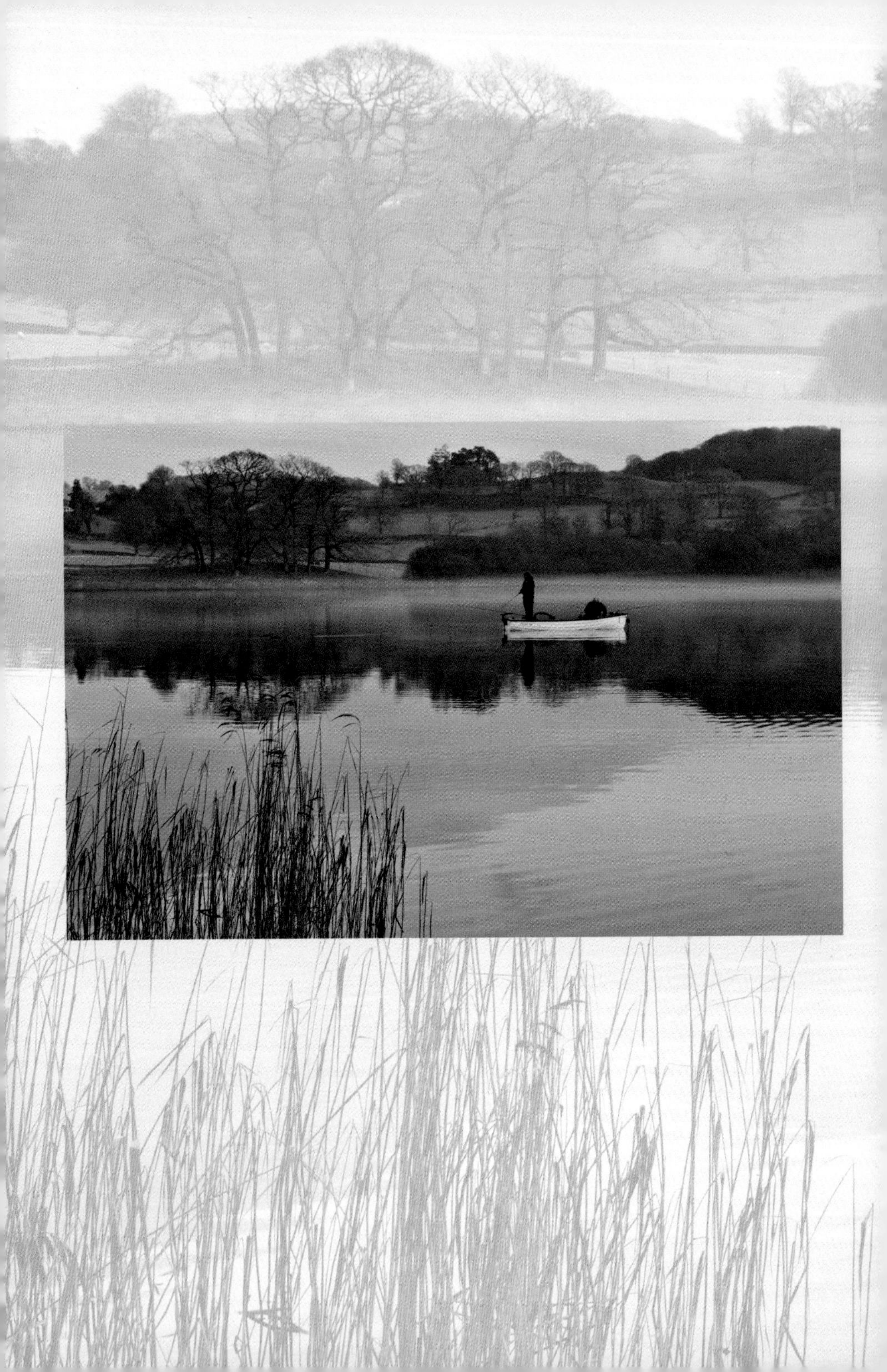

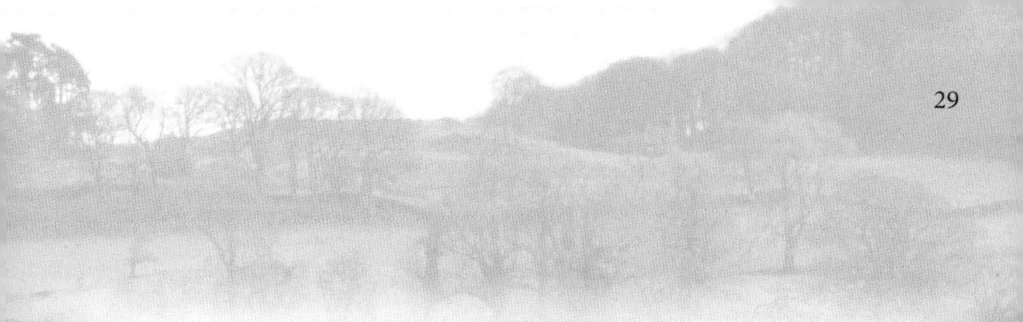

Friendship

I really like this photo. I gaze at it often, for it hangs on the wall of one of the corridors in Thornleigh House, where I live. It beckons me to silence and pondering. Esthwaite is one of the lesser-known lakes of Cumbria. It is situated near the town of Hawkshead, famous for its ferry across Windermere, and the fact that for a few years Wordsworth went to school there. He mentions this small lake in his 'Prelude' three times. Beatrix Potter had connections with this area, especially the small village of Sawry. As is clear from the photo, the lake is quite narrow. Usually, the visitors are few. The quality of this picture is enhanced, I feel, by the reeds in the foreground and the gentle layer of mist on the water. The group of trees opposite is eye-catching, the reflections quite sharp.

Here are two friends in a hired boat, enjoying the calm and peace, comfortable with each other's company, engaged in a spot of recreational fishing, clearly a shared interest. Friendship is such a wonderful experience, such a precious gift. A common interest can enhance its quality, as can the ability to be silent and still together. It was St Thomas Aquinas who wrote that the highest form of love is friendship. And the great Greek philosopher Aristotle maintained that without friends no one would want to live, even if possessing all the other good things of life. Let's beware of taking our friends for granted; let's be deeply grateful for the friends in our lives; let's seek to develop our capacity to be a good friend. And let's remember that Jesus once said: "You are my friends."

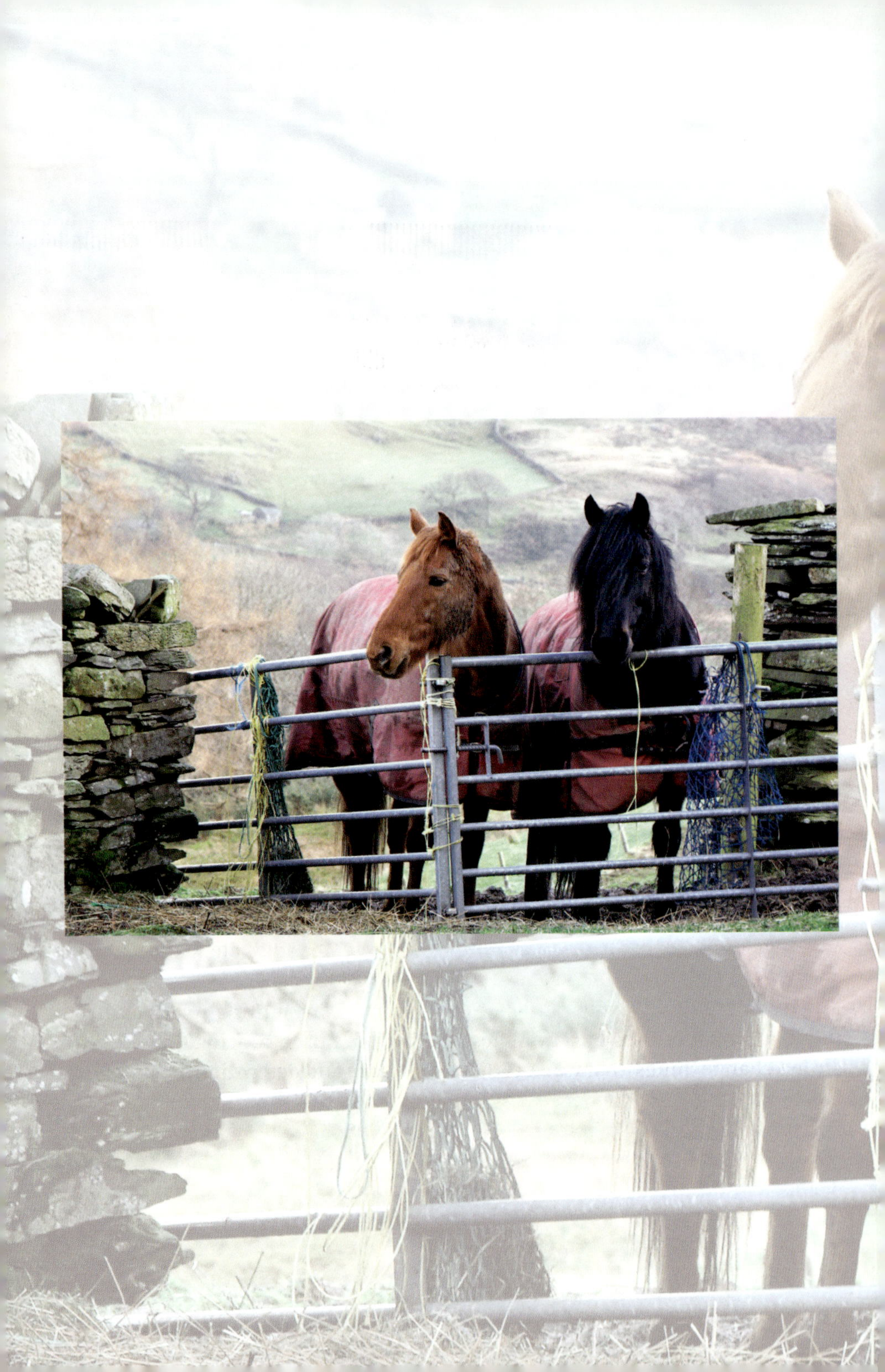

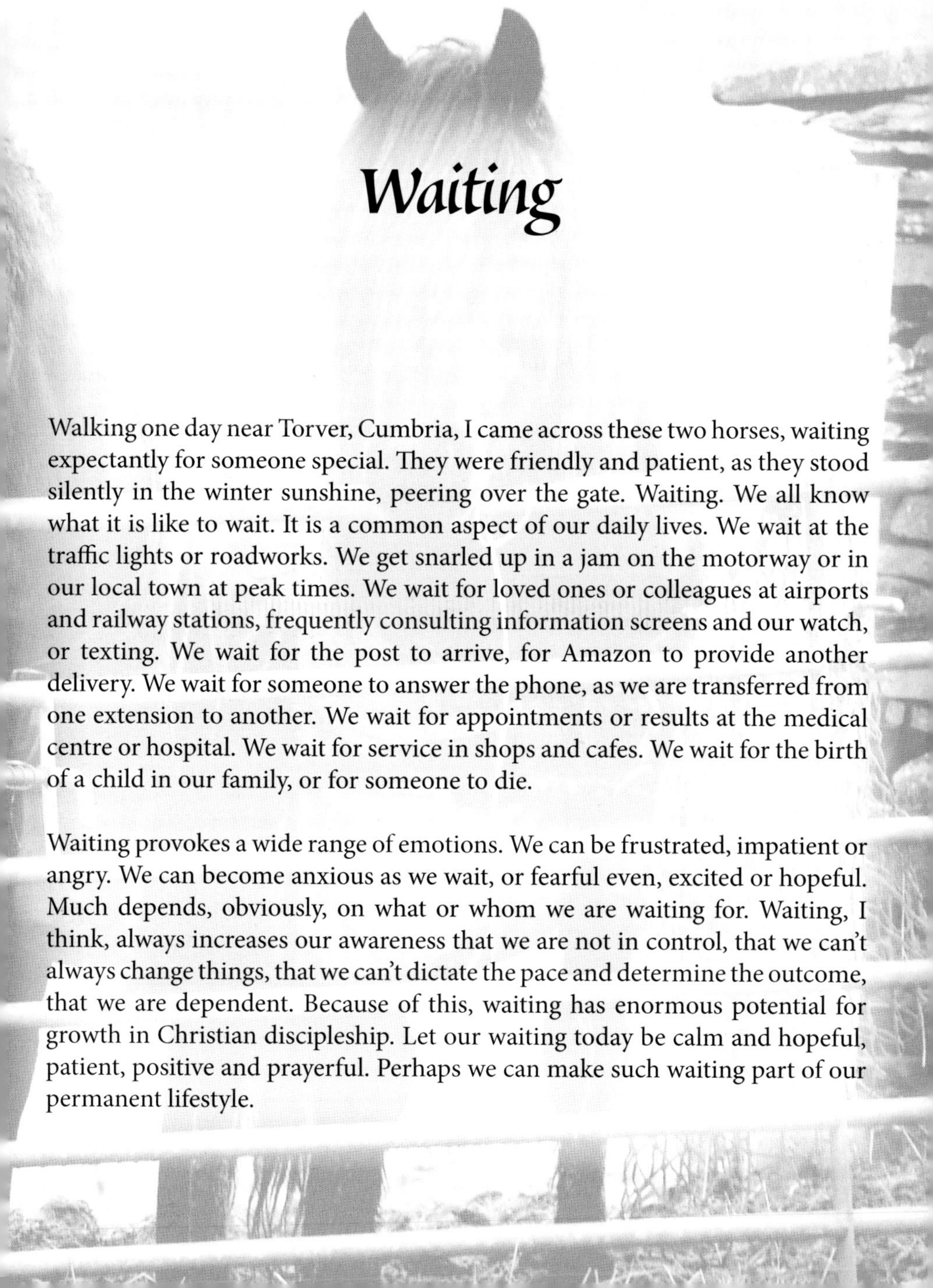

Waiting

Walking one day near Torver, Cumbria, I came across these two horses, waiting expectantly for someone special. They were friendly and patient, as they stood silently in the winter sunshine, peering over the gate. Waiting. We all know what it is like to wait. It is a common aspect of our daily lives. We wait at the traffic lights or roadworks. We get snarled up in a jam on the motorway or in our local town at peak times. We wait for loved ones or colleagues at airports and railway stations, frequently consulting information screens and our watch, or texting. We wait for the post to arrive, for Amazon to provide another delivery. We wait for someone to answer the phone, as we are transferred from one extension to another. We wait for appointments or results at the medical centre or hospital. We wait for service in shops and cafes. We wait for the birth of a child in our family, or for someone to die.

Waiting provokes a wide range of emotions. We can be frustrated, impatient or angry. We can become anxious as we wait, or fearful even, excited or hopeful. Much depends, obviously, on what or whom we are waiting for. Waiting, I think, always increases our awareness that we are not in control, that we can't always change things, that we can't dictate the pace and determine the outcome, that we are dependent. Because of this, waiting has enormous potential for growth in Christian discipleship. Let our waiting today be calm and hopeful, patient, positive and prayerful. Perhaps we can make such waiting part of our permanent lifestyle.

Our Heritage

Photographers speak of the 'blue hour' shortly after sunset. I suppose this image is an example, though I wasn't thinking of that at the time! This is the view of the Isle of Whithorn harbour, Galloway, taken from outside the cottage where we were staying for the week. Judging by the gulls near the pier, a fishing boat must have just come in. The harbour is a peaceful place, the villagers very warm and friendly. The remains of the chapel of Saint Ninian can be found there, dating back for centuries. A few miles along the coast is Ninian's cave, which is a pilgrimage venue.

In this photo, I'm captivated by the calm beauty of the place, due mainly to the light. There is also that fascinating mix of a modern world built on centuries of rich history. It's good, I believe, from time to time, to ponder our heritage, and acknowledge with gratitude those who have gone before us, on whose shoulders we now stand.

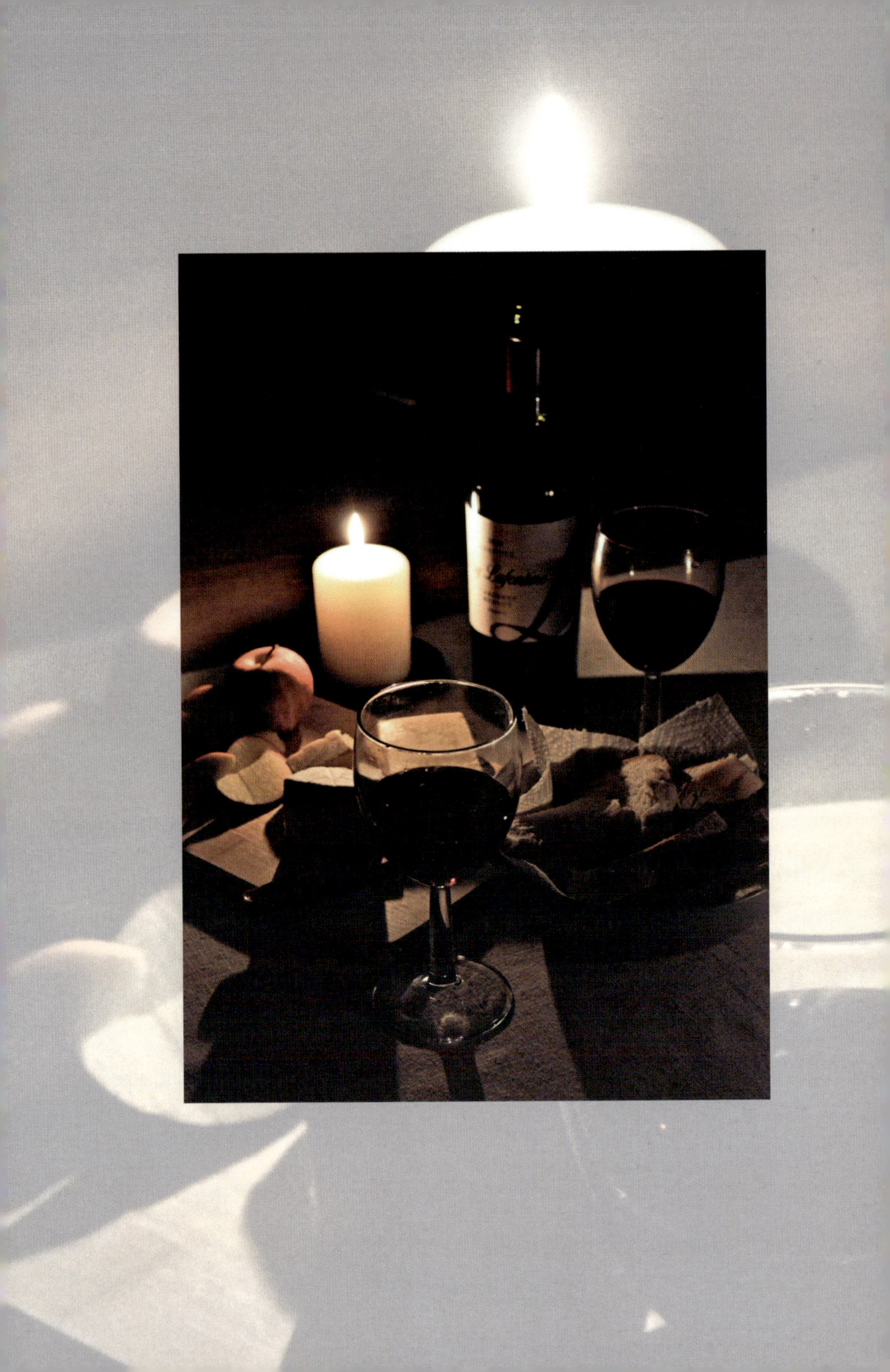

Celebrating Life

Technically, this photo would be considered, I believe, as 'still life'. The original situation fits that title, as there had been a power cut, so the preparation of the meal was on hold! Rather than hunt for candles, I chose an artistic enterprise. One of my confrères occasionally recalls an incident when, as a young brother returning from university one evening, he noticed a bottle of wine on the table. Asking the rector of the community what was being celebrated, he received the reply: "We are celebrating life, brother; life."

So today, let's think about celebrating: celebrating a particular person, a significant event or experience. Or let's simply celebrate life in all its mystery and wonder, and let's thank our God for all the blessings which life brings.

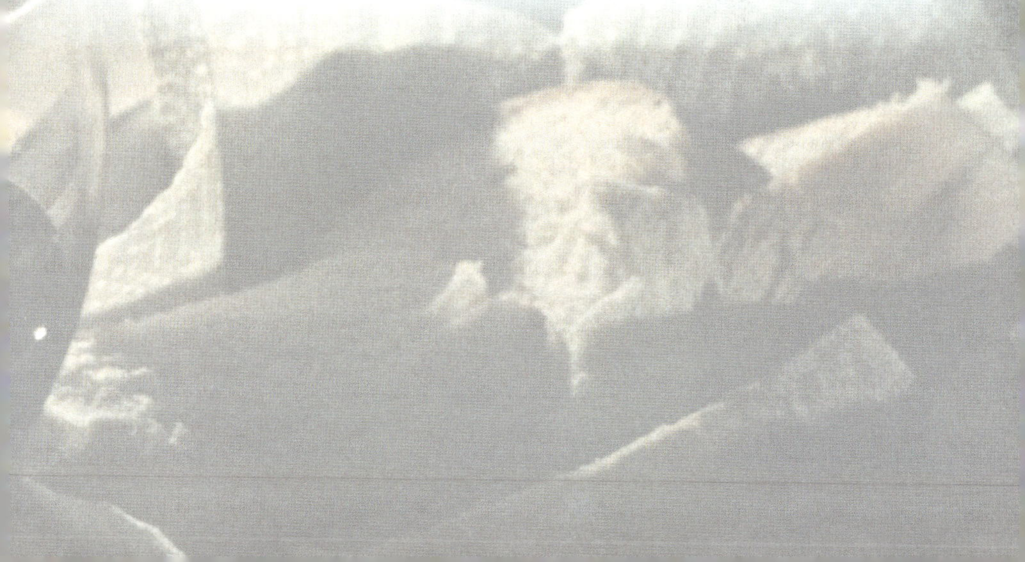

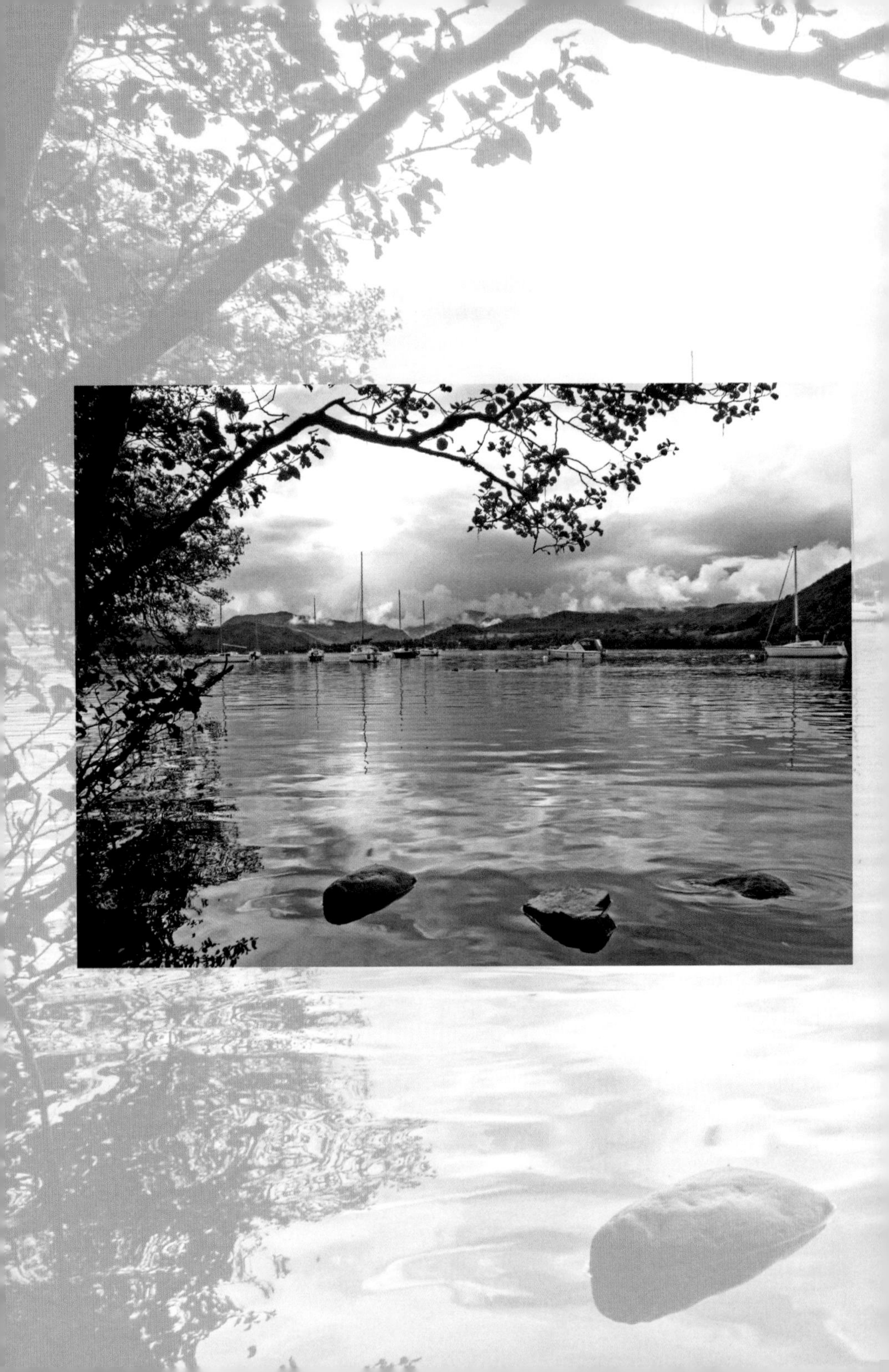

Calm After The Storm

People sometimes speak about the calm before the storm. This photo tells of the calm **after** the storm! I took it some time ago at Ullswater, near Pooley Bridge. There had been heavy rain earlier. The wind is clearly blowing the storm clouds away to engulf the Helvelyn massif, and is affecting the position of the boats and the surface of the lake. I think there is something magical about the water in the foreground with the reflections and the three small rocks. It seems to be pulling me in! And the air after the storm is bright and clear.

As is often the case, nature mirrors human experience, or is it the other way round? Difficulties arise often in our lives, problems of different kinds and intensities, storm-like. We struggle for a while, but often they pass, and a welcome calm returns. We probably thank God, and those who have helped us through the situation. The storm enhances our appreciation of returning calm and the inner peace which floods our spirit. In that peace, with clearer mind, we can reflect on what has happened and what we have learnt from the experience. Storms, though threatening, can lead to creativity and newness.

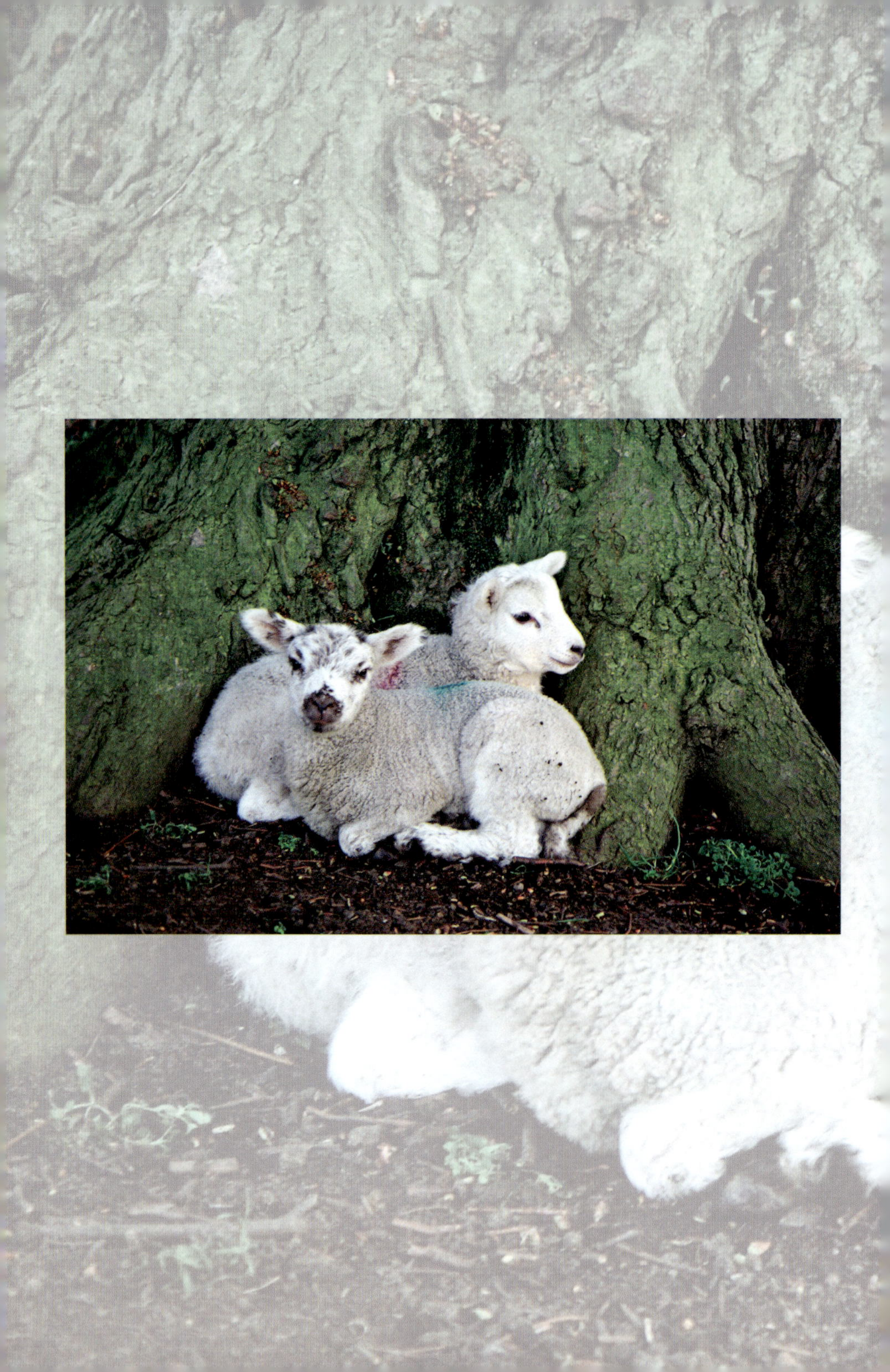

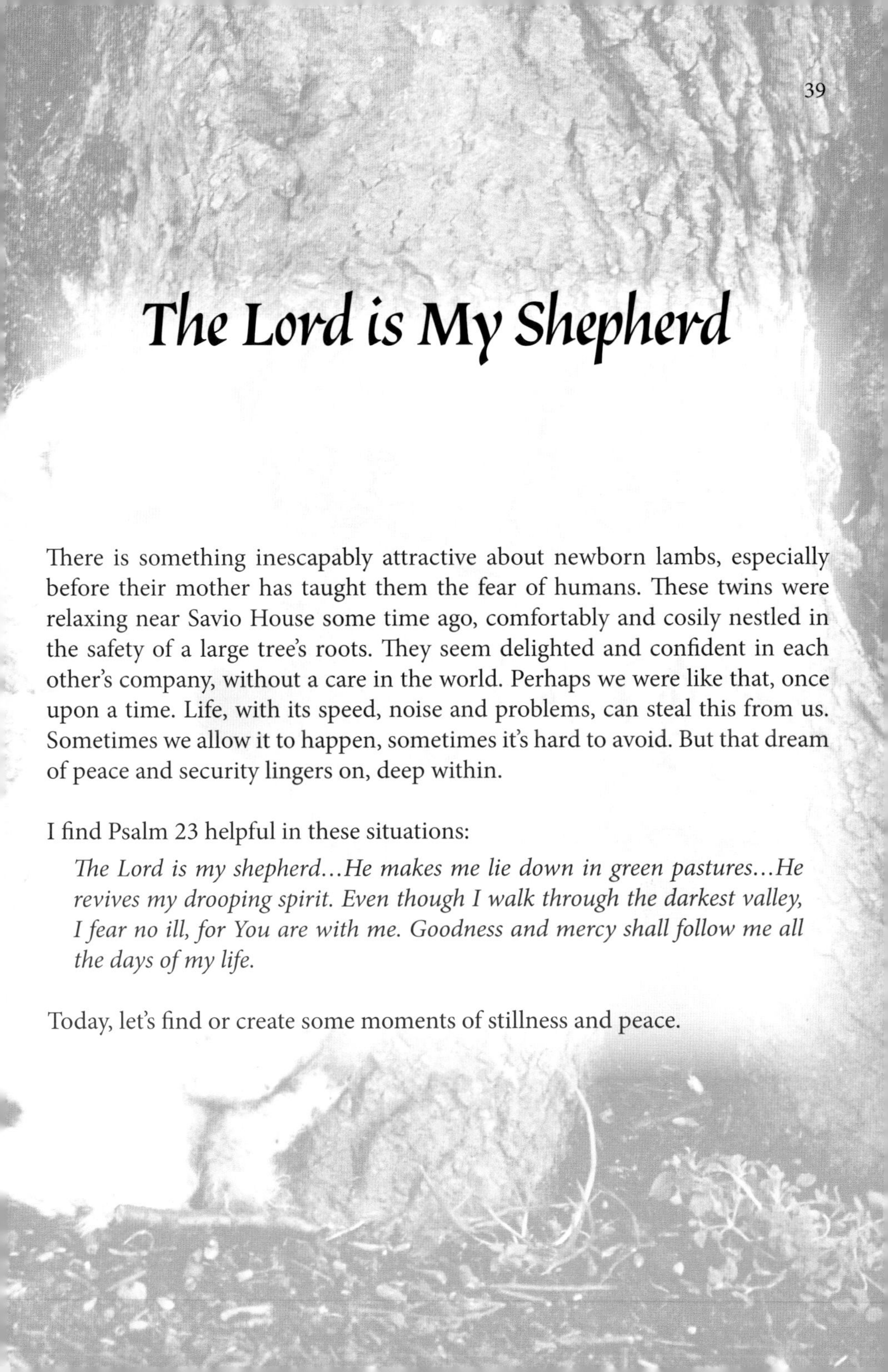

The Lord is My Shepherd

There is something inescapably attractive about newborn lambs, especially before their mother has taught them the fear of humans. These twins were relaxing near Savio House some time ago, comfortably and cosily nestled in the safety of a large tree's roots. They seem delighted and confident in each other's company, without a care in the world. Perhaps we were like that, once upon a time. Life, with its speed, noise and problems, can steal this from us. Sometimes we allow it to happen, sometimes it's hard to avoid. But that dream of peace and security lingers on, deep within.

I find Psalm 23 helpful in these situations:

> *The Lord is my shepherd…He makes me lie down in green pastures…He revives my drooping spirit. Even though I walk through the darkest valley, I fear no ill, for You are with me. Goodness and mercy shall follow me all the days of my life.*

Today, let's find or create some moments of stillness and peace.

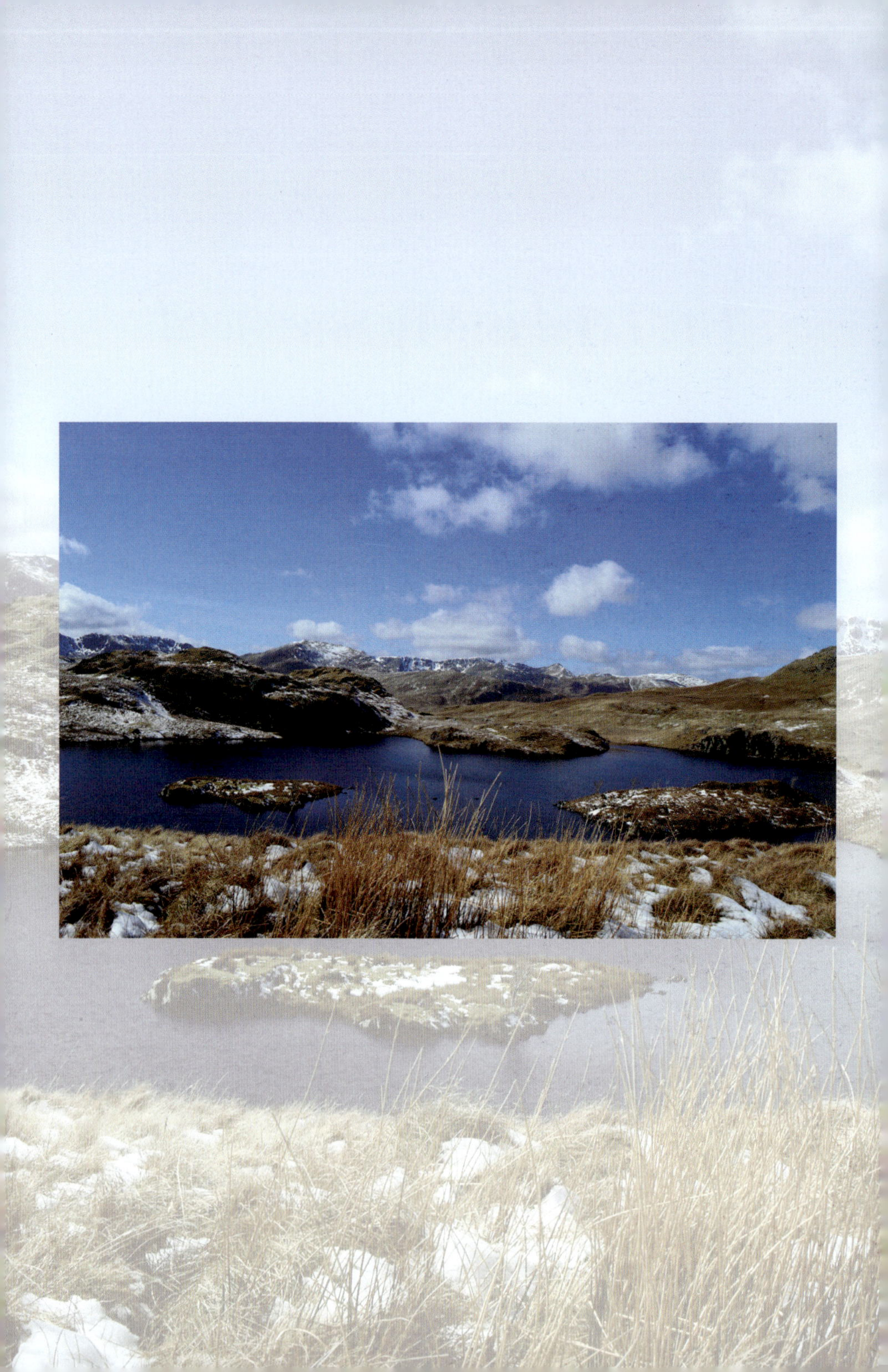

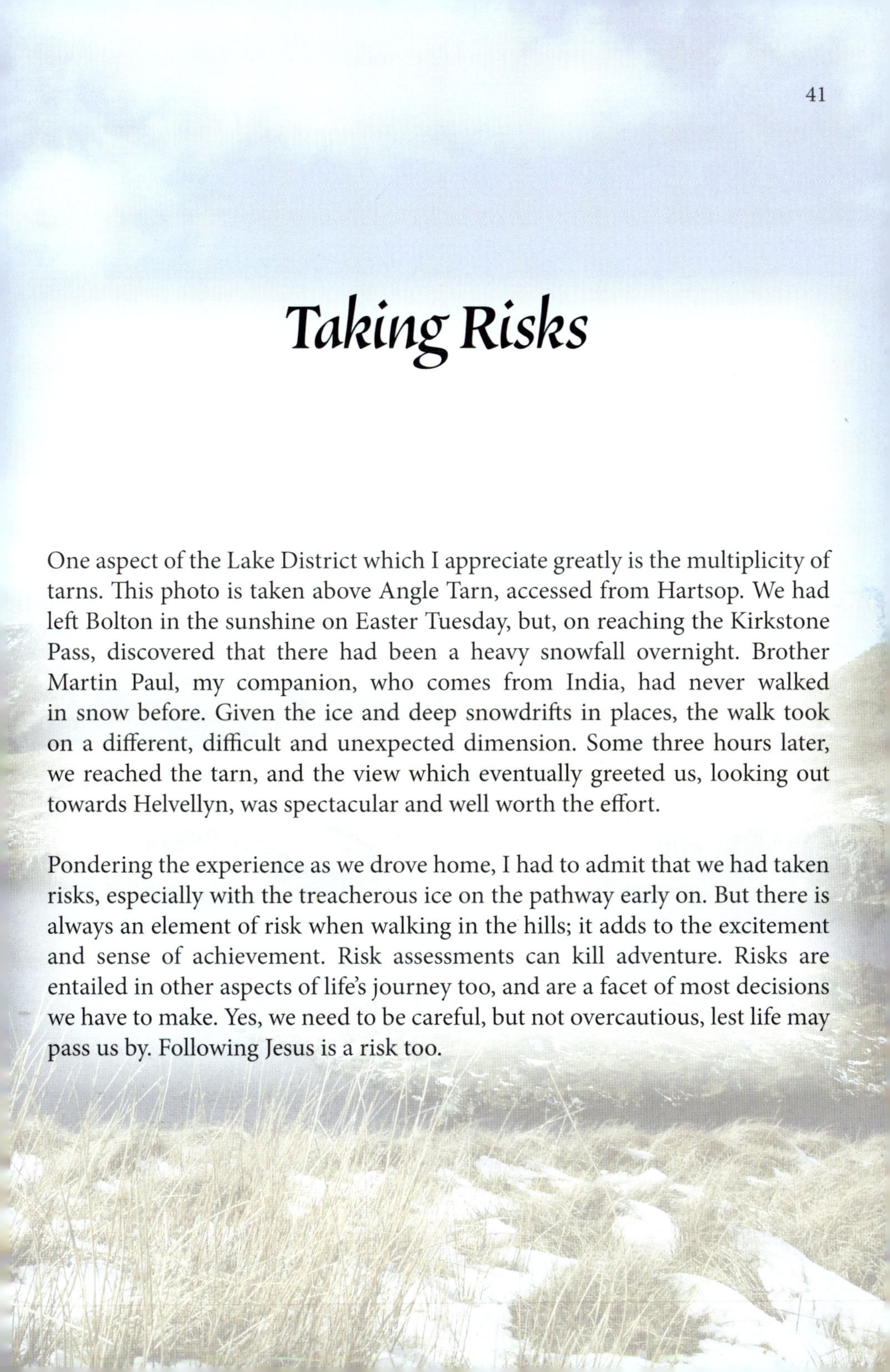

Taking Risks

One aspect of the Lake District which I appreciate greatly is the multiplicity of tarns. This photo is taken above Angle Tarn, accessed from Hartsop. We had left Bolton in the sunshine on Easter Tuesday, but, on reaching the Kirkstone Pass, discovered that there had been a heavy snowfall overnight. Brother Martin Paul, my companion, who comes from India, had never walked in snow before. Given the ice and deep snowdrifts in places, the walk took on a different, difficult and unexpected dimension. Some three hours later, we reached the tarn, and the view which eventually greeted us, looking out towards Helvellyn, was spectacular and well worth the effort.

Pondering the experience as we drove home, I had to admit that we had taken risks, especially with the treacherous ice on the pathway early on. But there is always an element of risk when walking in the hills; it adds to the excitement and sense of achievement. Risk assessments can kill adventure. Risks are entailed in other aspects of life's journey too, and are a facet of most decisions we have to make. Yes, we need to be careful, but not overcautious, lest life may pass us by. Following Jesus is a risk too.

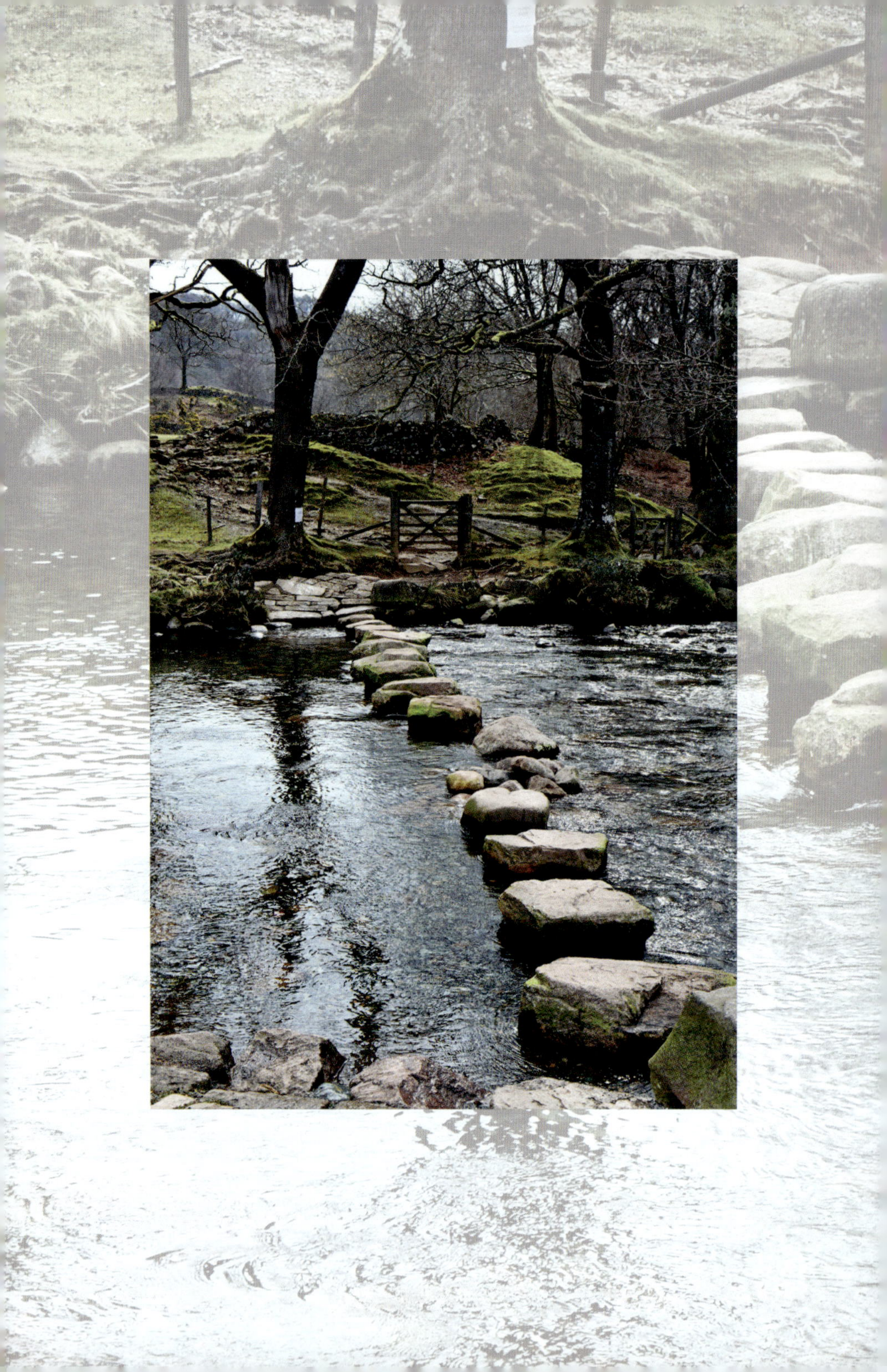

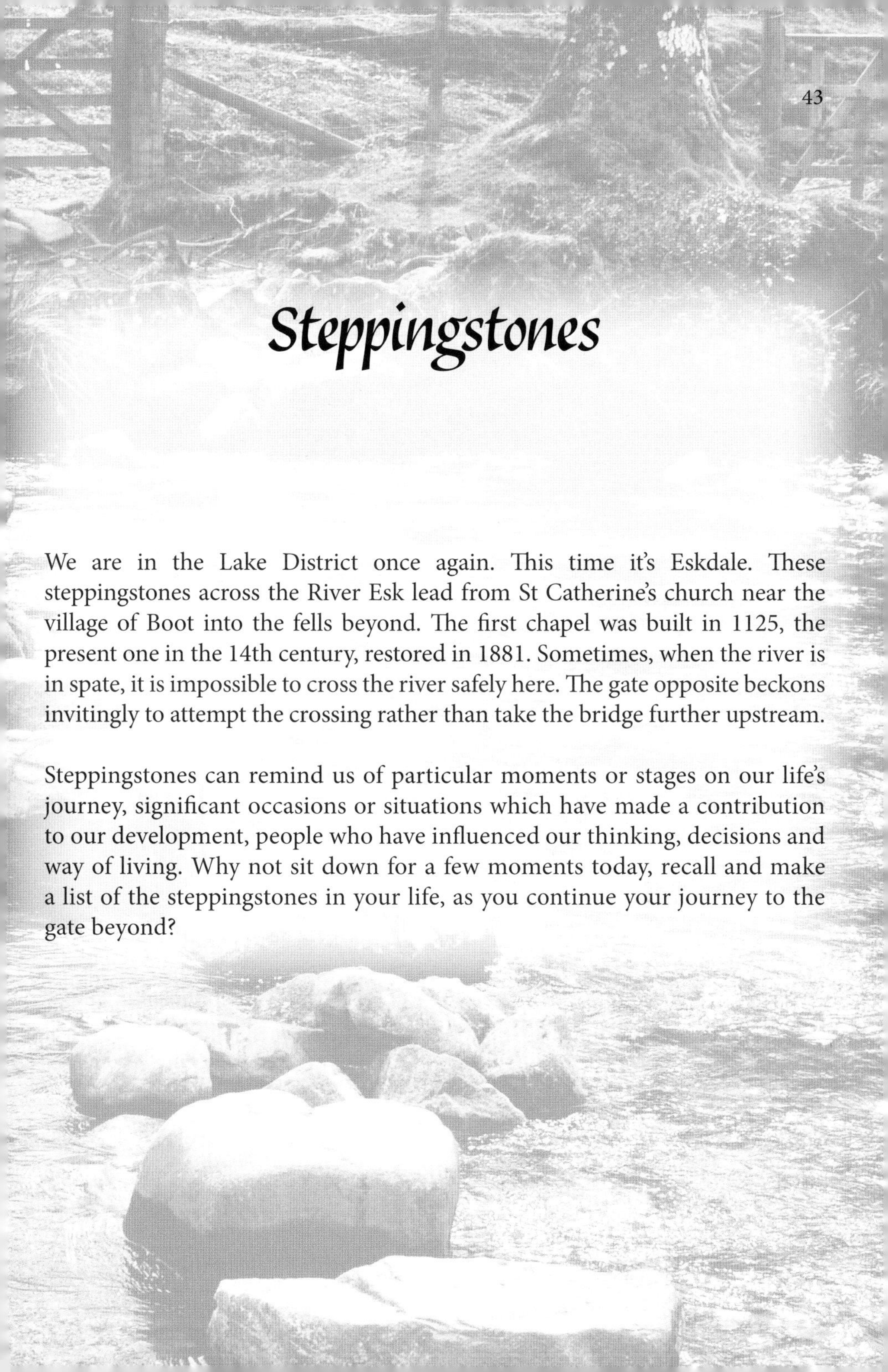

Steppingstones

We are in the Lake District once again. This time it's Eskdale. These steppingstones across the River Esk lead from St Catherine's church near the village of Boot into the fells beyond. The first chapel was built in 1125, the present one in the 14th century, restored in 1881. Sometimes, when the river is in spate, it is impossible to cross the river safely here. The gate opposite beckons invitingly to attempt the crossing rather than take the bridge further upstream.

Steppingstones can remind us of particular moments or stages on our life's journey, significant occasions or situations which have made a contribution to our development, people who have influenced our thinking, decisions and way of living. Why not sit down for a few moments today, recall and make a list of the steppingstones in your life, as you continue your journey to the gate beyond?

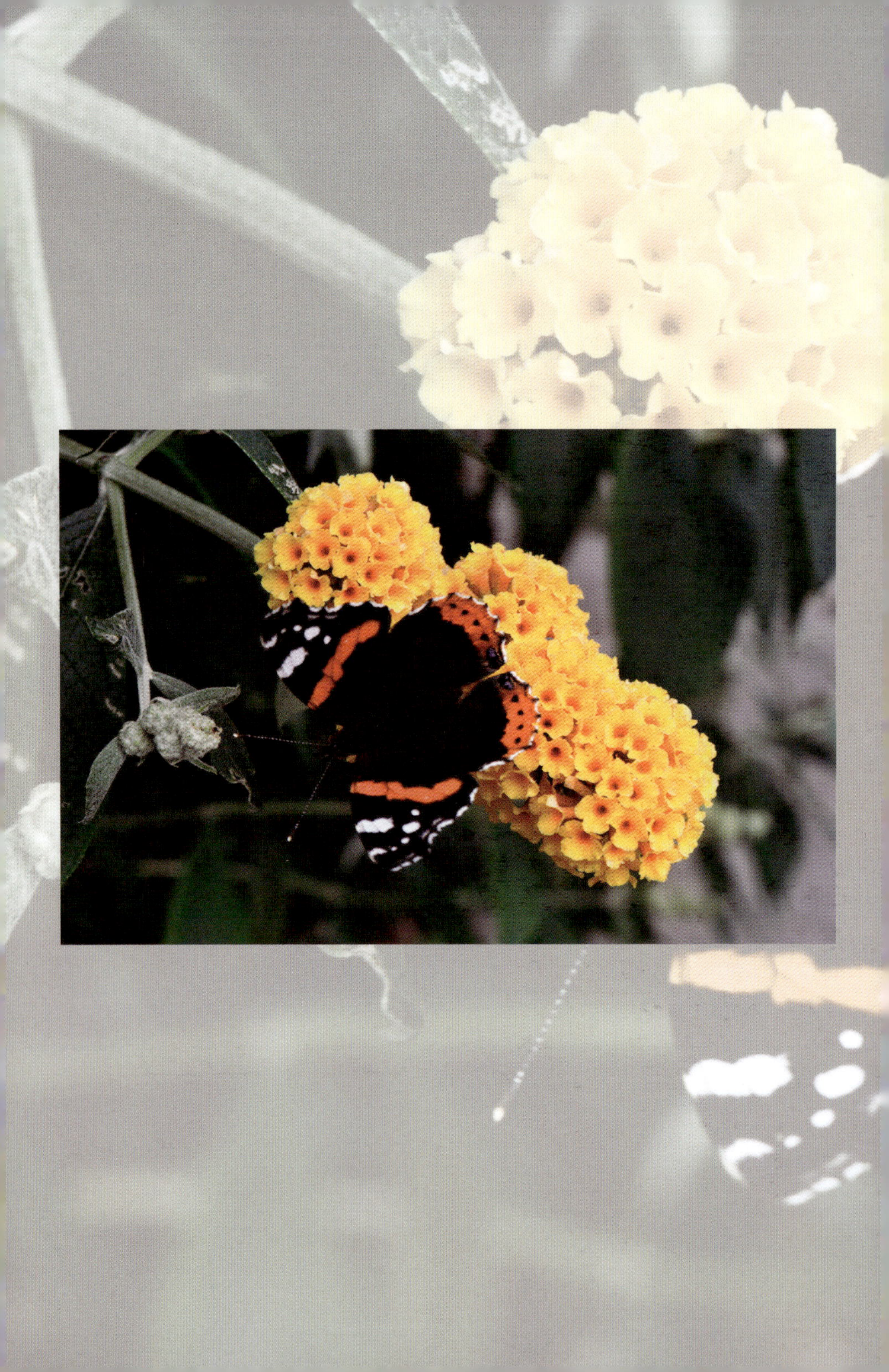

Nature's Free Gifts

Butterflies are such attractive little creatures. They come into our lives initially as a sign of the arrival of spring. And that gives a little jolt of joy. Usually, they flit around busily, moving on if they become aware of human attention. Sometimes it is possible to get really close and catch a photo without needing a zoom lens. In this image I do like the contrast with the yellow flower. I'm not sure what it is. Buddleia is a butterfly favourite, but is usually purple in colour; it is often referred to as a 'Butterfly Bush'. There are many native butterflies; this is a Red Admiral; the markings are spectacular and easy to recognise. I'm intrigued by the antennae. Isn't nature marvellous? Sadly, eight species are now endangered.

I previously referred to a flower as a 'smile from God'. I think a butterfly is a similar smile. It certainly always brings a smile to my face, and my eyes instinctively seek to follow its flight. Butterflies are a lifeform of colour, beauty, restless movement, unaided by us humans, and therefore are one of nature's free gifts. For this we are grateful, and we do not take them for granted.

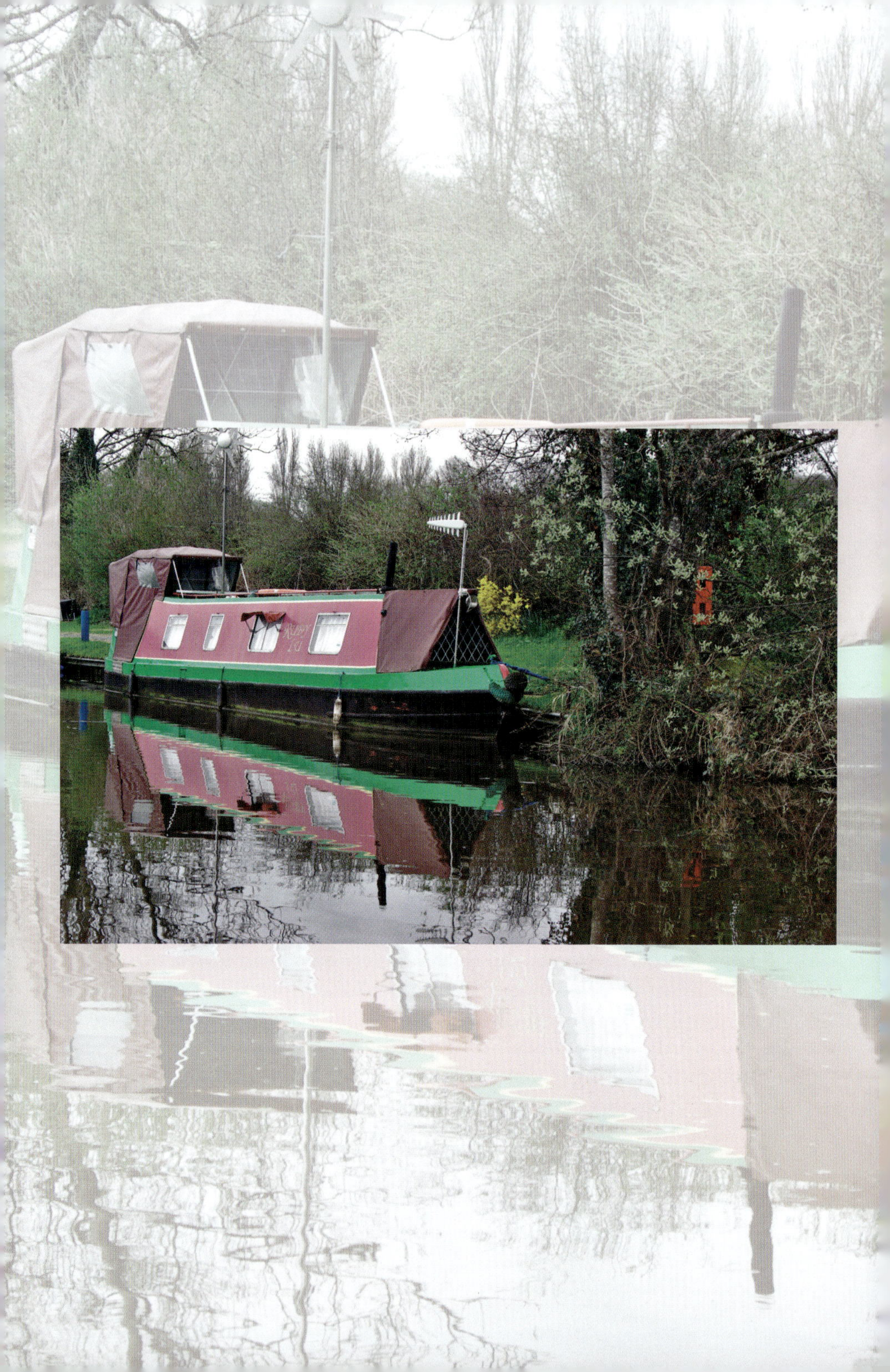

Appreciating Alternatives

Canals are fascinating places. In Roman times they were used for irrigation. Here in the UK, an amazing network of some 4000 miles was developed during the industrial revolution, constructed for the transporting of materials and goods like coal and iron ore; they were an important part of industrial development. The advent of the railway reduced their use considerably. In recent years, they have come to be used for recreational purposes, with many people buying attractively designed barges for gentle cruises. Some people actually live in them, a version of mobile homes. Originally, barges were pulled by horses, so most canals have a path alongside the waterway. Nowadays these provide opportunities for walking and cycling. Very often the water is still, and so reflections are easy to capture, as in this photo. In some places, there are quite large marinas serving as bases for a large number of barges.

Perhaps barge people are like bikers, a kind of subculture enriching our life experience by highlighting originality and diversity. I think it's wonderful the way in which human beings create different ways of embracing the gift of life, and explore alternative possibilities. Even though I'd find travelling along at 5mph rather frustrating, I can see how it must be relaxing, even exciting, for others. Negotiating locks, however, must be quite a challenge. I think it's important for us to be able to welcome and appreciate diversity, not to be locked into sameness and glued into our comfort zones. Are there 'alternatives' which you struggle with? Can you become more open?

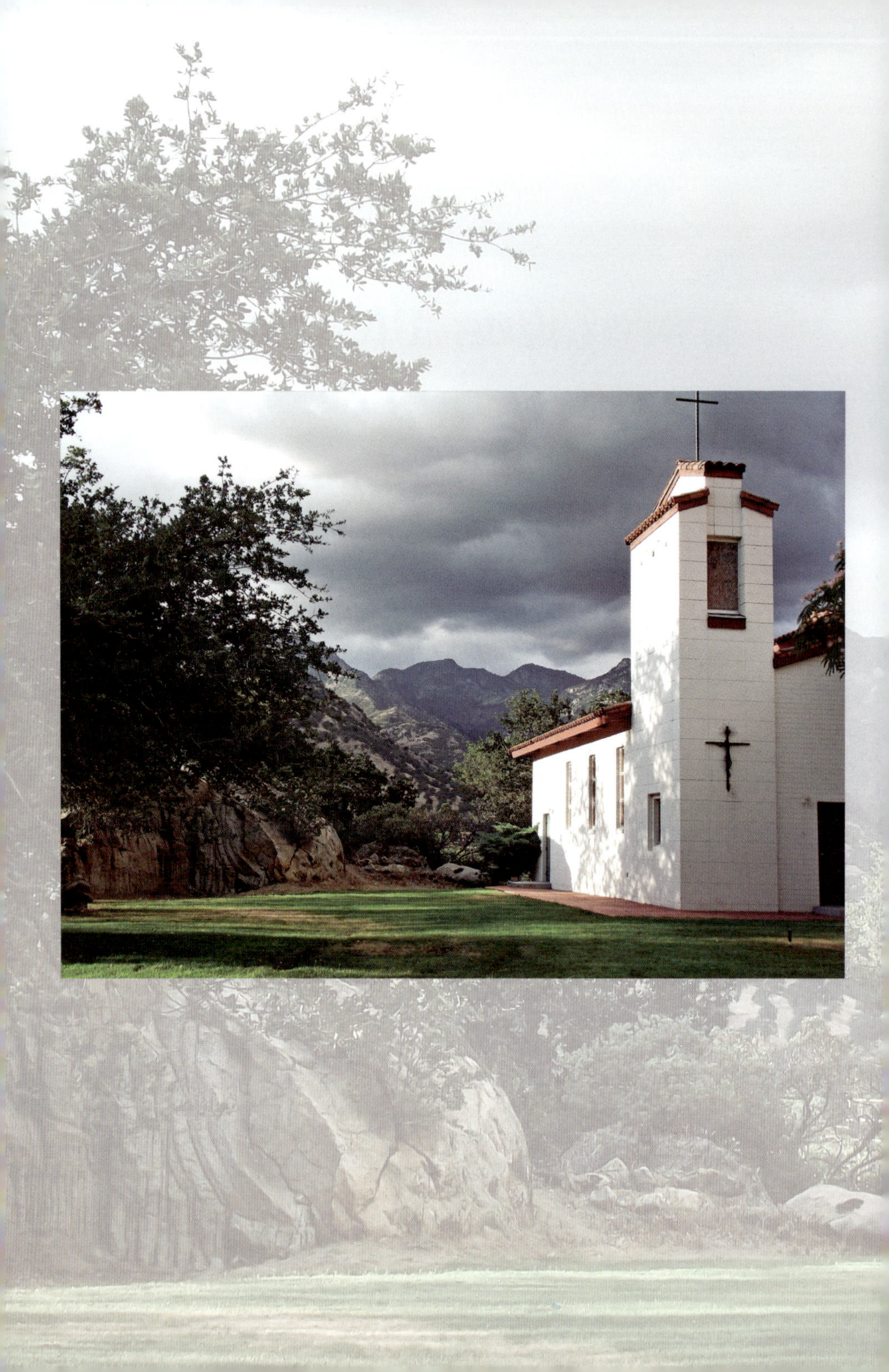

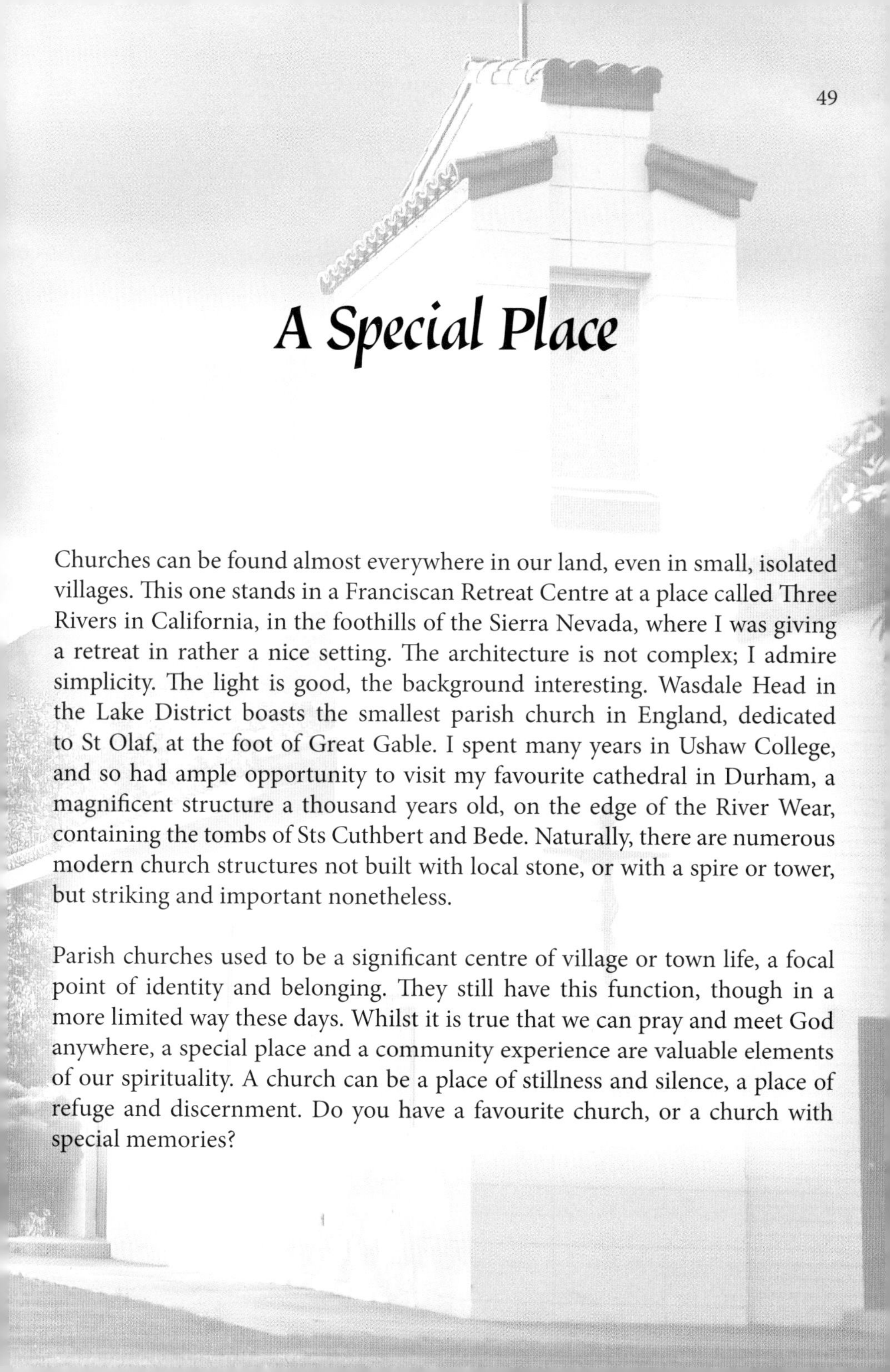

A Special Place

Churches can be found almost everywhere in our land, even in small, isolated villages. This one stands in a Franciscan Retreat Centre at a place called Three Rivers in California, in the foothills of the Sierra Nevada, where I was giving a retreat in rather a nice setting. The architecture is not complex; I admire simplicity. The light is good, the background interesting. Wasdale Head in the Lake District boasts the smallest parish church in England, dedicated to St Olaf, at the foot of Great Gable. I spent many years in Ushaw College, and so had ample opportunity to visit my favourite cathedral in Durham, a magnificent structure a thousand years old, on the edge of the River Wear, containing the tombs of Sts Cuthbert and Bede. Naturally, there are numerous modern church structures not built with local stone, or with a spire or tower, but striking and important nonetheless.

Parish churches used to be a significant centre of village or town life, a focal point of identity and belonging. They still have this function, though in a more limited way these days. Whilst it is true that we can pray and meet God anywhere, a special place and a community experience are valuable elements of our spirituality. A church can be a place of stillness and silence, a place of refuge and discernment. Do you have a favourite church, or a church with special memories?

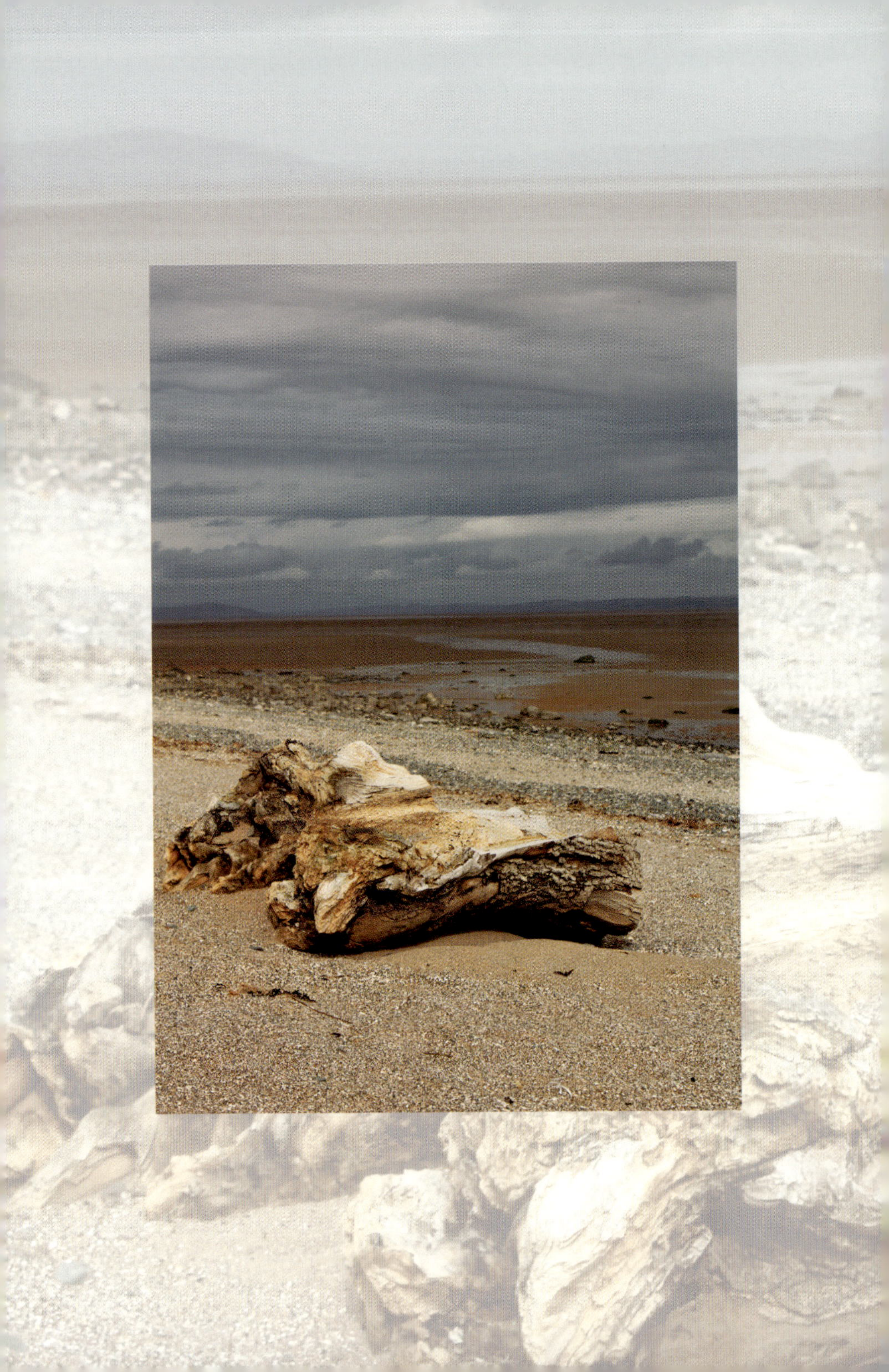

Driftwood

A common feature when walking along a shoreline after high tide is the sight of pieces of driftwood. I can't honestly say that this log just caught my eye; it couldn't be missed! We are at the edge of Morecambe Bay, near Newbiggin, just off the Ulverston-Barrow road. When the tide has receded, the bay is an enormous stretch of sand. After walking out for twenty minutes, one experiences a wonderful sense of aloneness, such a contrast with normal urban existence. There is so much empty space all around; one feels a speck in the universe, yet unique and special.

The texture of the driftwood log, chiselled by the elements, is fascinating. Where did this tree grow? Was it toppled by a storm or by human beings? How old was it when it came to die? How did it reach the sea, and where? It was probably part of the lives of many people over decades. If it could talk, what stories would it tell? Thinking about it, I feel a great oneness, a kinship with the natural world of which we are a part. Do you feel one with nature in its manifold forms?

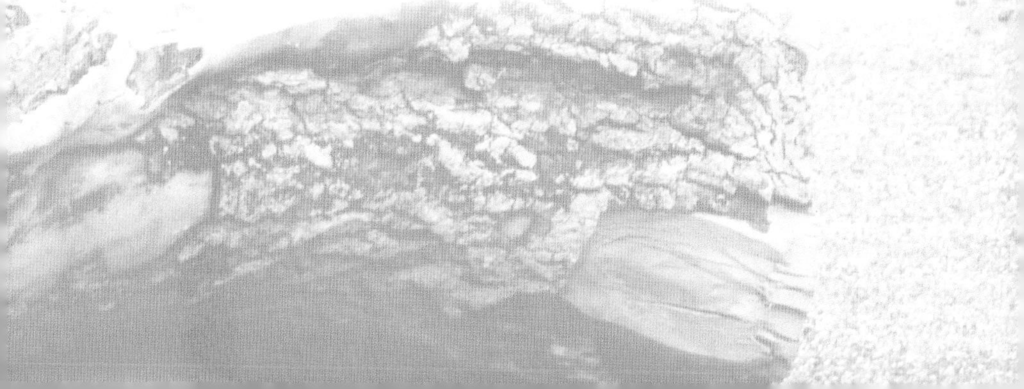

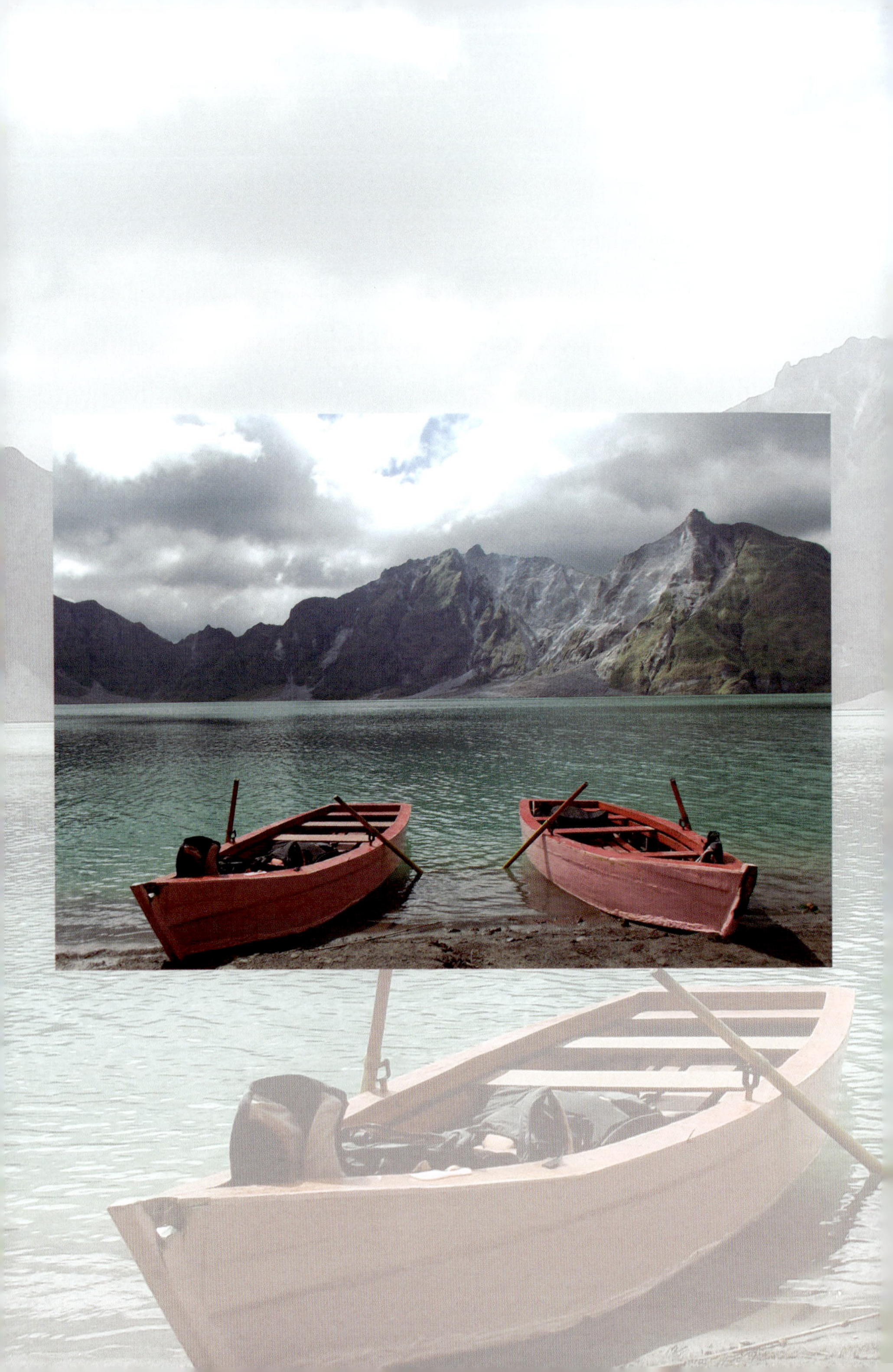

Rebuilding

Some years ago, I spent five months with the Salesians in the Philippines at their Centre for Theological studies in Parañaque, Manila. During the Christmas break, a small group of them kindly invited me to accompany them to Lake Pinatubo. Until about twenty years previously (1991) Pinatubo was a beautiful volcano. Then it erupted with spectacular and devastating effect. More devastating still was the mudflow a couple of years later after very heavy typhoon rainfall. By the time of our visit, Pinatubo had become a tourist attraction, accessible on foot after an exhilarating jeep ride. The deep blue water in the crater lake was still quite warm. The others had a swim before we took the boats to the other side. The scars from the eruption are evident and convey a vivid sense of the power of the volcano, yet nature is gradually reclaiming its territory.

Sometimes volcanic eruptions can occur in our lives, like failure, separation, the death of a loved one. Events can leave lasting scars. The challenge is learning gradually how to cope and rebuild our lives. For this we need help, perhaps professional, certainly from friends, and we need faith in God's presence and love.

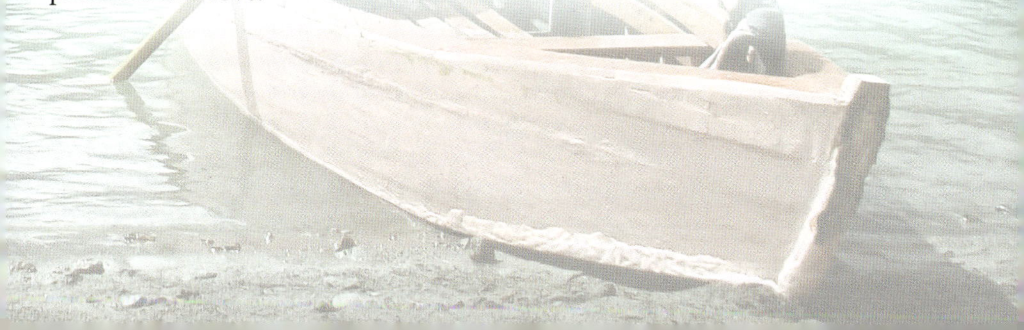

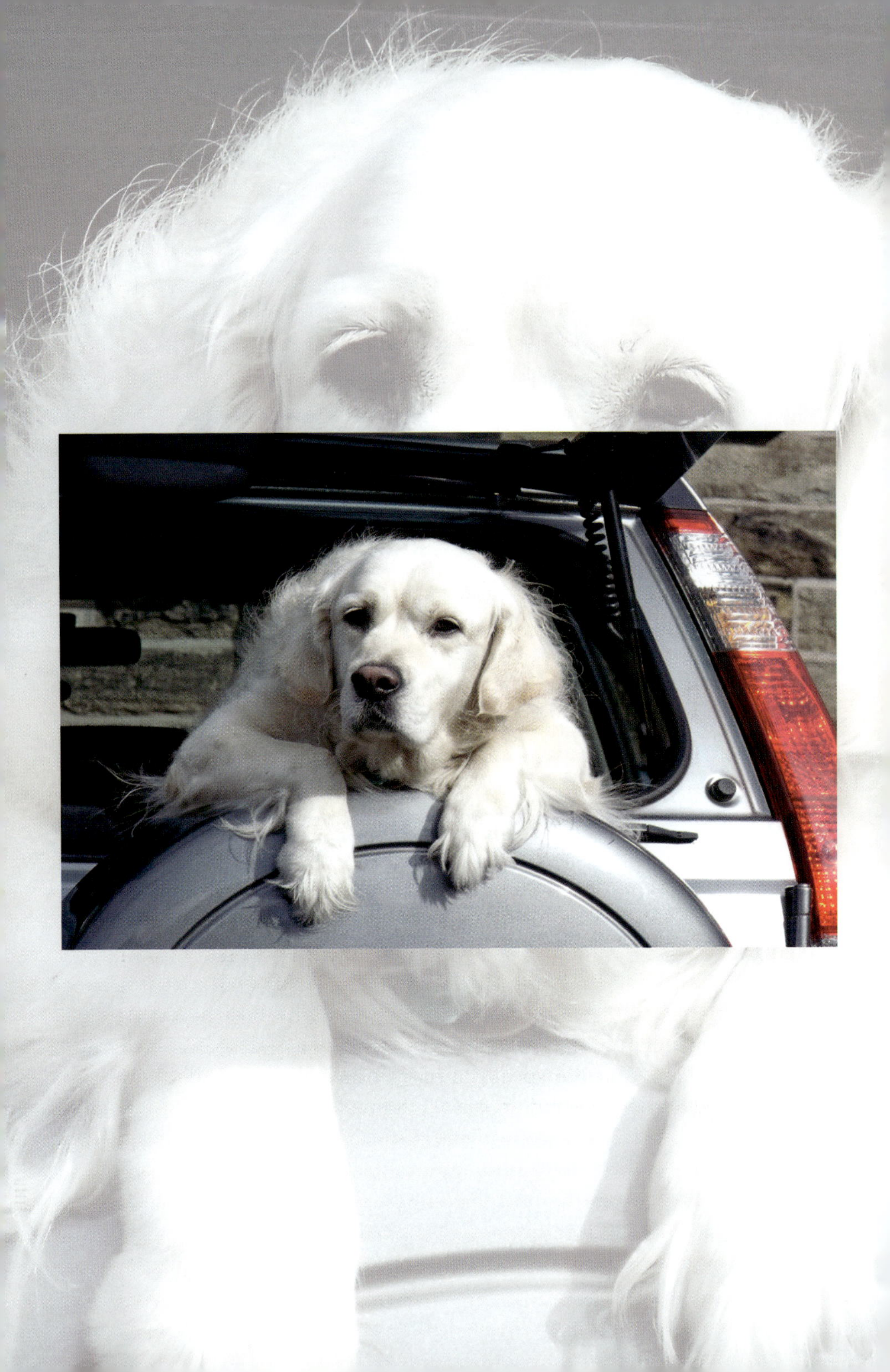

God Sees Us

In recent years, I have come to appreciate Labradors and Retrievers. They are wonderful animals and faithful friends. This one, Zac by name, belonged to Margaret and Martin who for many years worked with us at Savio House, our residential youth retreat centre near Macclesfield. Zac frequently took refuge in the boot of their car, seeking to avoid the attentions of the young people visiting the centre who found him irresistible. He would sit there just quietly surveying the situation.

Don Bosco used to have a poster on the wall of his early oratories which stated: ‘God sees you’. In my youth I interpreted this as a warning to be good, to avoid misbehaviour. The God I had in mind was a finger-waving, harsh God, not easy to love. In my later ministry, I’ve come across many adults whose image of God is similarly negative. But Zac offers an alternative way of understanding that motto of Don Bosco. Certainly, Zac misses nothing, but his watchful gaze is calm, gentle, friendly, affirming. I always felt that Zac was on my side, not looking to catch me out. I believe our God is like that, as Jesus tells us. Perhaps today we could reflect on our image of God; is it really the God of Jesus? Paul Tournier speaks of his “all-inclusive, unconditional love, his unreserved acceptance and approval”.[1] Some find this difficult to believe; but such an understanding of God can be so liberating, and can transform our lives.

---

1 P. Tournier, *Guilt and Grace*, (London: Hodder & Stoughton, 1962), 189.

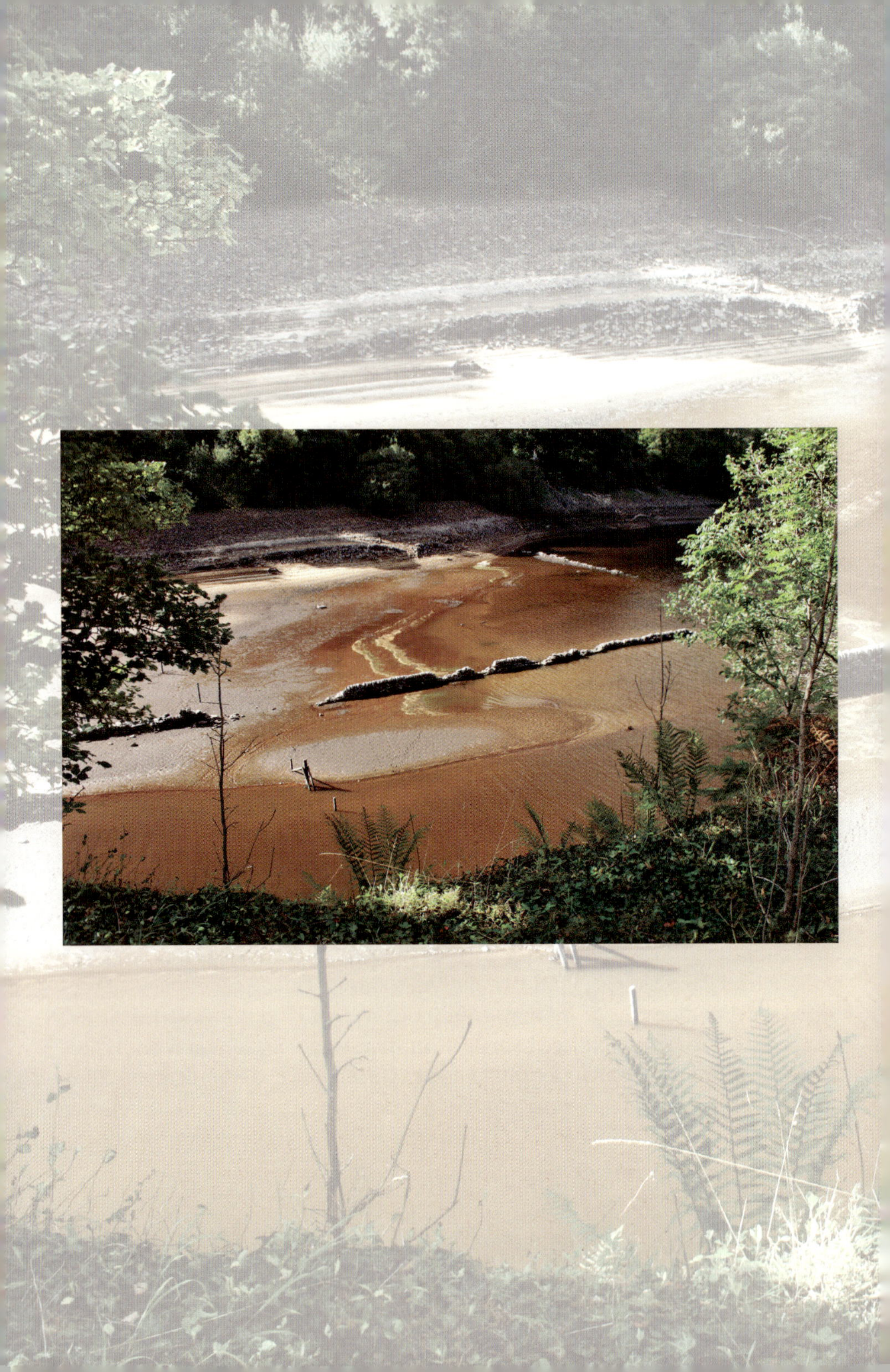

Gratitude

Recently, I visited Goyt Valley. It was a trip of nostalgia, for it is a place I often walked and enjoyed when based in Savio House. In the valley there are two reservoirs: Fernilee, constructed in the 1930s; and Errwood, built in the later part of the 1960s. They both provide drinking water for Stockport and its environs. Because of the drought this year, the scene was almost unrecognisable. The photo captures the current bleak situation of Fernilee. Before construction began, the people living and working in the valley were relocated, which was no doubt a traumatic experience for them. The walls in the photo are relics of that earlier era. The people of Stockport have long benefitted from their forgotten sacrifice.

The current state of the reservoir reminds us of the environmental challenges we face, and is perhaps a particular challenge to be more careful with our use of water and avoiding waste. The history of the reservoir encourages us to be grateful not only for our water supply, but also for the sacrifices of those whose lives were radically changed through reservoir construction, for what happened at Fernilee has happened in many places in our land, and the drought conditions we have recently been experiencing has highlighted these past events.

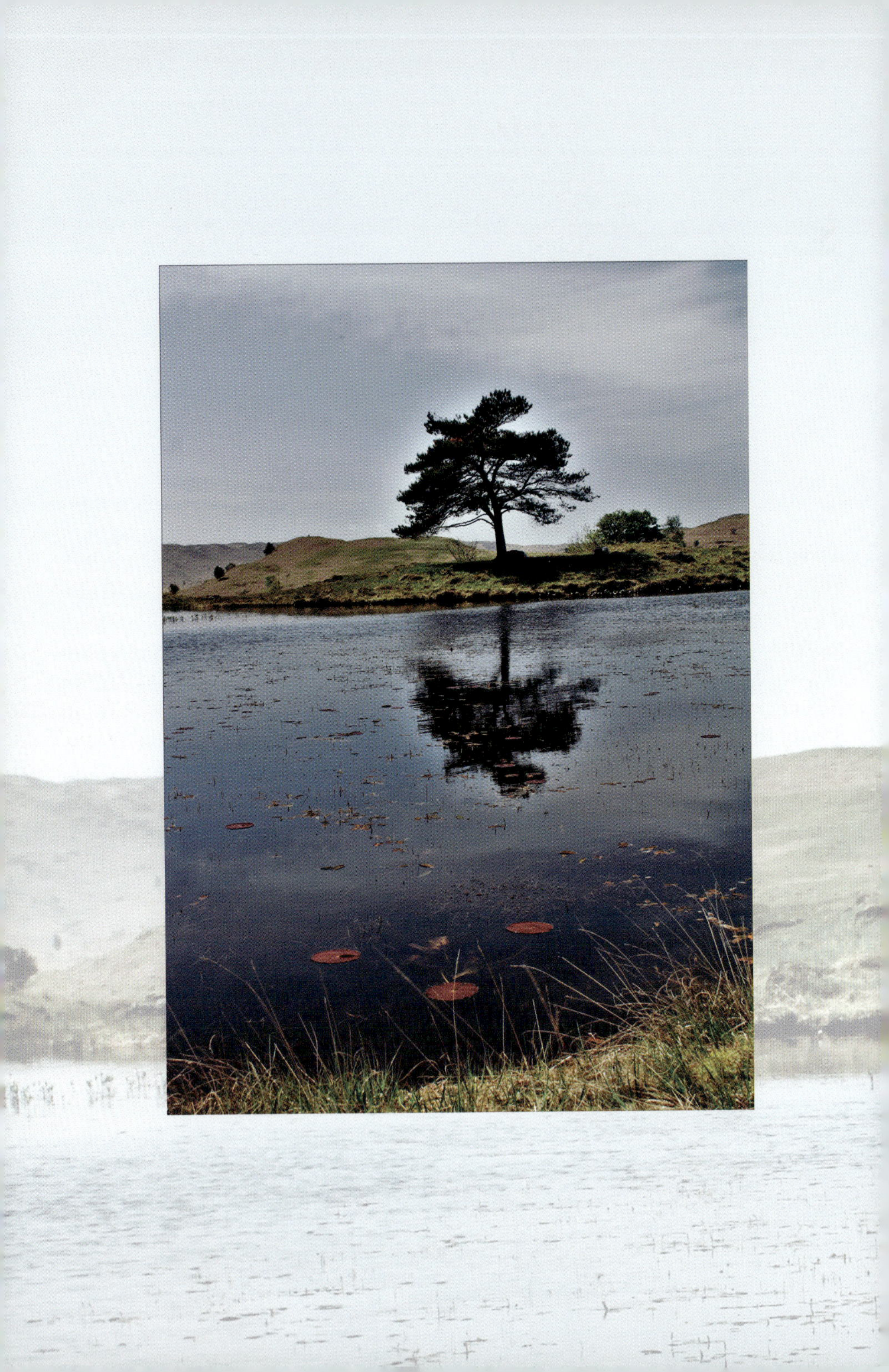

Alone with God

Trees! How wonderful they are. As human beings, we seem to have an affinity with our trees, and we share some characteristics. Some are old, wizened and gnarled. Others are youthful and bright. Some are tall and graceful, others small or chaotic. Some are very beautiful, others less so. Some stand with others in a woodland, others alone in a field. In winter you can appreciate the intricacy of branch formation, in autumn the wonderful tapestry of colour; in spring the delicate coming to new life; in summer the canopy of green. Many photographers wax eloquently about trees, and I have been sucked into their enthusiasm. I'm aware of always being on the lookout for the isolated tree, the lone tree. This photo was taken at Kelly Tarn, near Torver. I don't think this lone tree would be quite so beautiful without the water of the tarn, which adds charm and variety to the scene.

Today, let's really notice the trees we pass, and thank God for them. Maybe we could stop and stare. Can we identify with any of them? I wonder what my love for the lone tree is saying about me at this stage in my life! I recall a song about the tree which looks at God all day and lifts its leafy arms to pray. If a tree can help us pray today, it will be a further enrichment to our life.

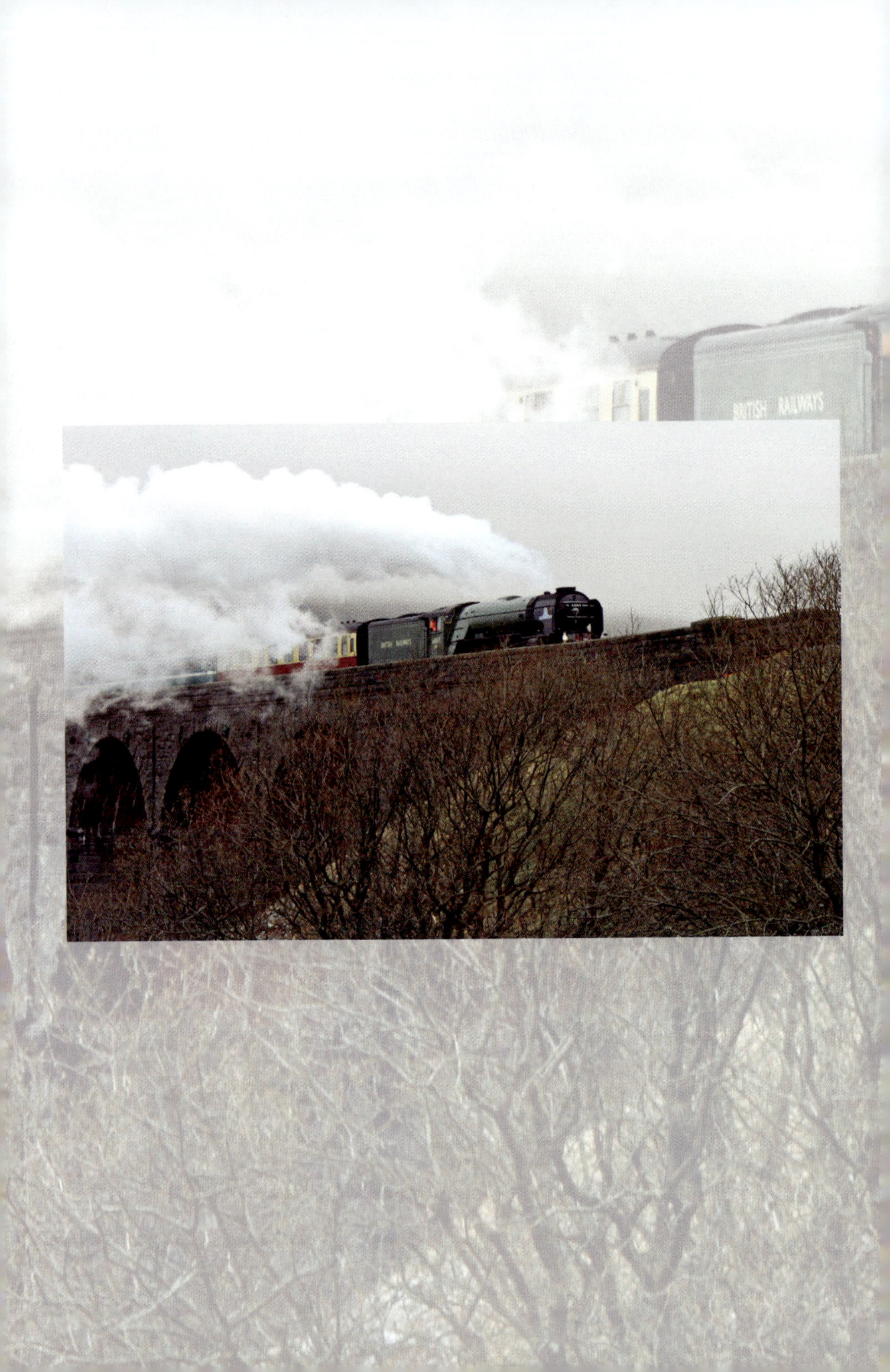
BRITISH RAILWAYS

Excitement of Learning

As a boy, I was a keen trainspotter. On a Saturday, I would buy a 1 penny platform ticket and spend hours on Wigan NW station with many other young people, Ian Allan booklet in hand, noting down the numbers and names of the many trains which stopped there or thundered through, rocking the platform. Of course, in those days the engines were steam-driven, and had a power and noisy excitement unrivalled by later diesel and electric trains. In 2018 during the February midterm break, a new locomotive, built by enthusiasts, plied the route from Settle to Carlisle and back just for a few days, pulling several passenger-filled carriages. This was an opportunity not to be missed, and the best place for a photo was undoubtedly the Ribblehead viaduct. So off I went, though in the process I fell heavily and hurt my shoulder, which troubled me for several months. But it was worth it!

It's interesting how childhood enthusiasms don't wane with age. As parents and educators it is important to foster such interests in our young people, to broaden their minds to the many facets of being alive in our world. I always find it heartening when I meet parents with young children walking the fells, or I see young people learning to canoe or sail. I remember once at 11,000 feet in the Val d'Aosta encountering children of four or five years of age learning how to ski! There is always something exciting about learning something new, or enabling others to do so. It's part of being fully alive, which is our calling from our God. What hobbies or skills did you learn when you were young? What are you now passing on to other young people?

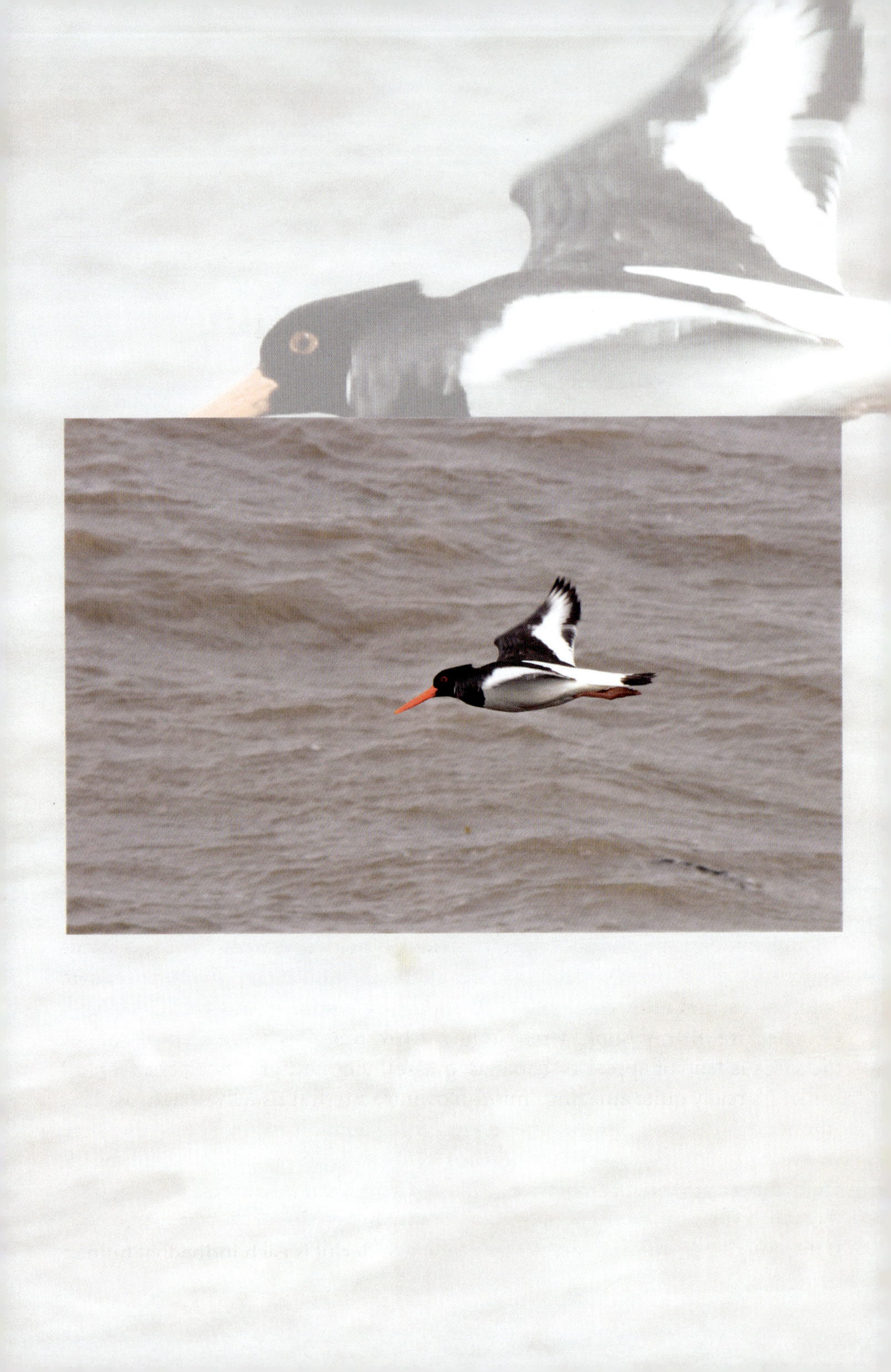

God's Extravagance

The magazine I receive each month has taught me that bird photography is a specialised genre. It suggests that enthusiasts need to know about the habits and habitats of the birds they are interested in, and then have available a long zoom lens and lots of patience. I have neither! Sitting in a 'hide', waiting for a bird to turn up, is as bad as going fishing, which I gave up decades ago! However, from time to time a bird will invite me to make a portrait, and it isn't difficult to oblige. This photo was taken on Roa Island in the boatyard, where I was sitting on a rock gazing at the sea. A few oystercatchers zoomed in, and, fortunately, I had the camera ready. These attractive birds spend winter here, and frequent Morecambe Bay, where cockles are quite an industry. They are quite bright, cheery, colourful and live for many years. The oldest on record reached forty!

One thing which has struck me frequently over recent years is nature's abundance. Though oystercatchers don't visit my native Wigan, over the years I have become aware of the amazing variety of birds in the UK. Likewise, I'm interested in wildflowers, and even within COVID lockdown restraints, I noted 120 locally. On checking in my book, I realise how many varieties there are. Of course, the same is true of apples or bananas, grasses, vineyard grapes, tigers, tropical fish… It's really quite amazing, 'mind-blowing' (a term I usually seek to avoid!). Abundance! Jesus was into abundance too: twenty gallons of wine at Cana, twelve baskets of leftovers after feeding thousands. There is something lavish about God's love for us, extravagant even. Duns Scotus wrote about *haeceitas,* the 'thisness' of things; each blade of grass has its own identity and uniqueness. If this is true of birds and wildflowers, how wonderful is each individual human being within God's abundance. And that means you and me.

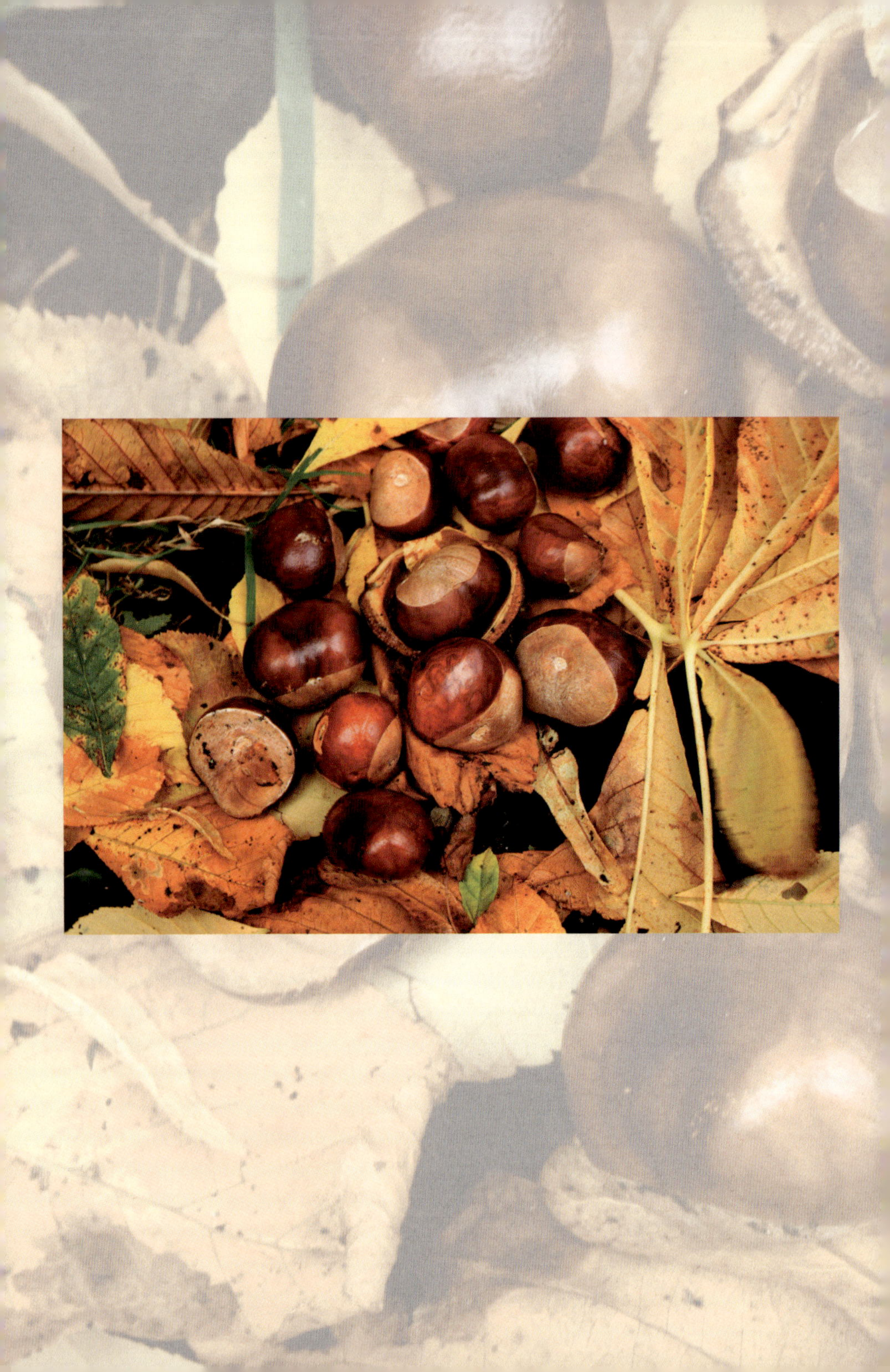

Lavish Nature

Whilst we adults tend to associate autumn with stunning colours, for children it has a different connotation: conkers. The fruit of the Horse Chestnut tree, the conker, provided much entertainment and competition when we were young, and cunning ways of hardening them for the fray were devised. I recently came across a grandfather and grandson hunting for a supply on the land of Savio House, our youth retreat centre, and was delighted. I believe that the sport of conkering is now frowned upon in the school playground for health and safety reasons!

For the older generation, these nuts have a brightness, beauty and variety of their own, standing out against the background of beech and chestnut leaves. Isn't nature wonderful and generous each year in producing leaf and nut and the possibility of fresh life for the future? Let's embrace this giftedness with humble gratitude today, and also seek to imitate it in our own lives.

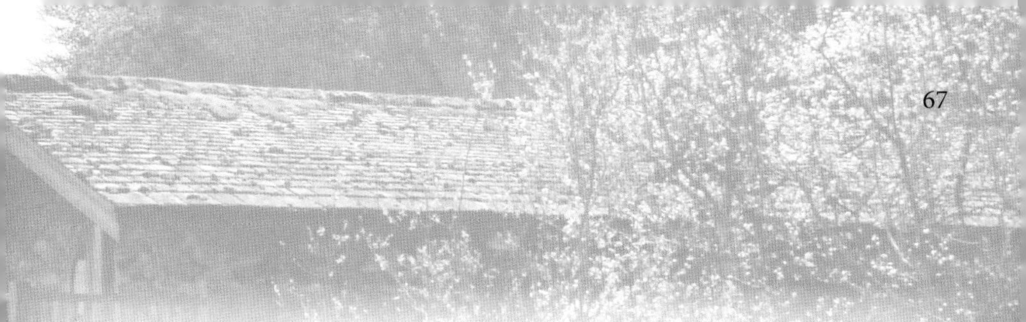

Embrace Your Originality

In recent years, I've come to realise that for most landscape photographers some images are a 'must have'. This boathouse, the 'Duke of Portland Boathouse', by the roadside near Pooley Bridge at the northern end of Ullswater, is one of them. I think the unusual little balcony must have something to do with its popularity, and the background of distant hills. Although lots of people take shots of places like this, none will be the same. Many factors contribute to the taking of a photo: weather conditions and time of year; light and the position of the sun; the orientation of the camera; the foreground and other compositional aspects; the angle of view, and so on. So even if the basic idea isn't original, there is a level of originality in the outcome.

I suppose these two factors can apply to countless things in our lives. Many areas of our lives and experiences are shared by others: most people have been educated, get married and have children; live in a house or flat; have a job; maybe have a garden and car; take holidays; go shopping; like music; follow a football team… the list goes on. And yet none is exactly the same. Each person's story is unique; we are all original creations. Difference and uniqueness are special and enriching. So, embrace your originality today and rejoice in it, even when you are doing what most others are doing, or what you do on a regular basis.

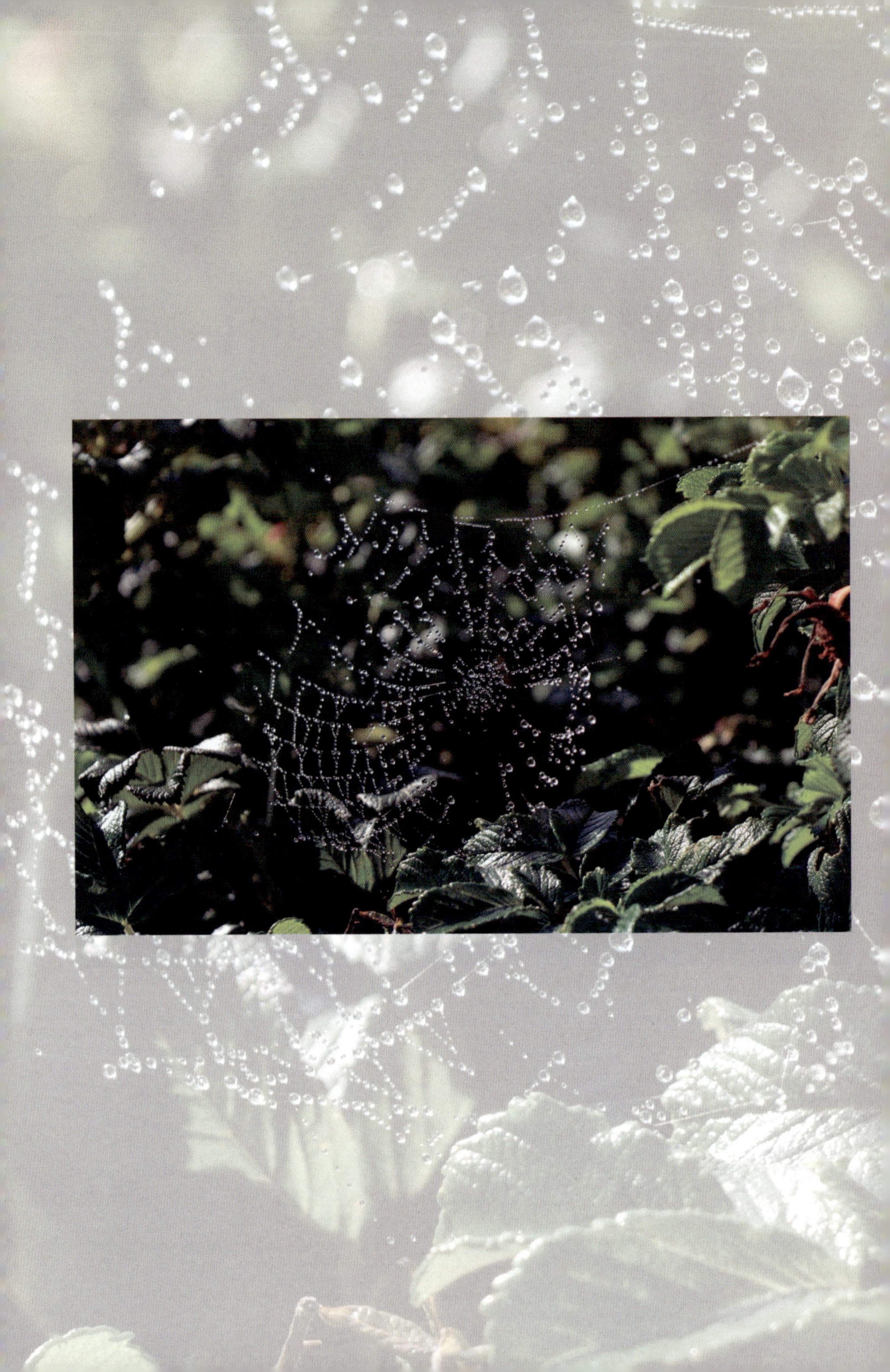

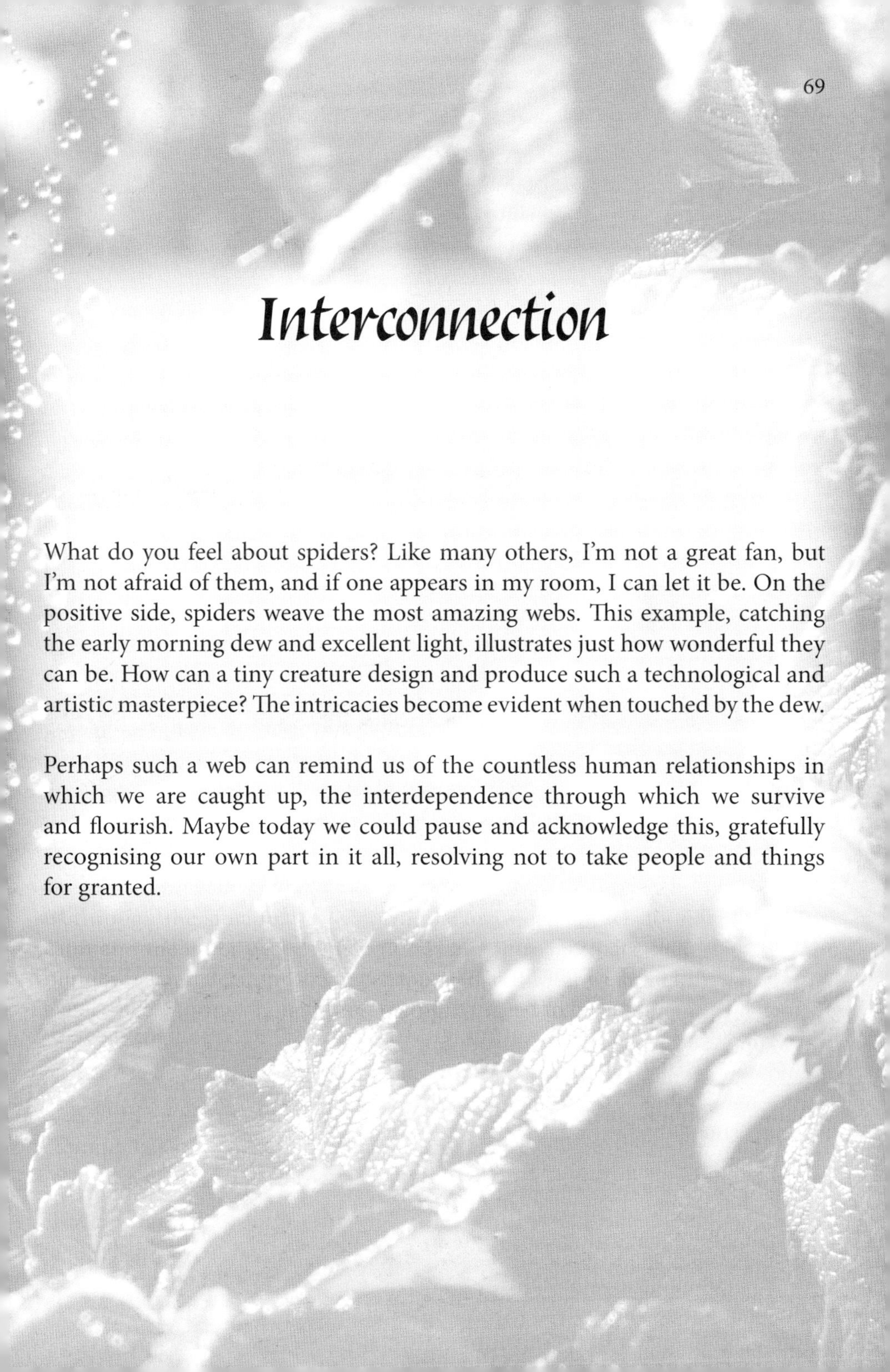

Interconnection

What do you feel about spiders? Like many others, I'm not a great fan, but I'm not afraid of them, and if one appears in my room, I can let it be. On the positive side, spiders weave the most amazing webs. This example, catching the early morning dew and excellent light, illustrates just how wonderful they can be. How can a tiny creature design and produce such a technological and artistic masterpiece? The intricacies become evident when touched by the dew.

Perhaps such a web can remind us of the countless human relationships in which we are caught up, the interdependence through which we survive and flourish. Maybe today we could pause and acknowledge this, gratefully recognising our own part in it all, resolving not to take people and things for granted.

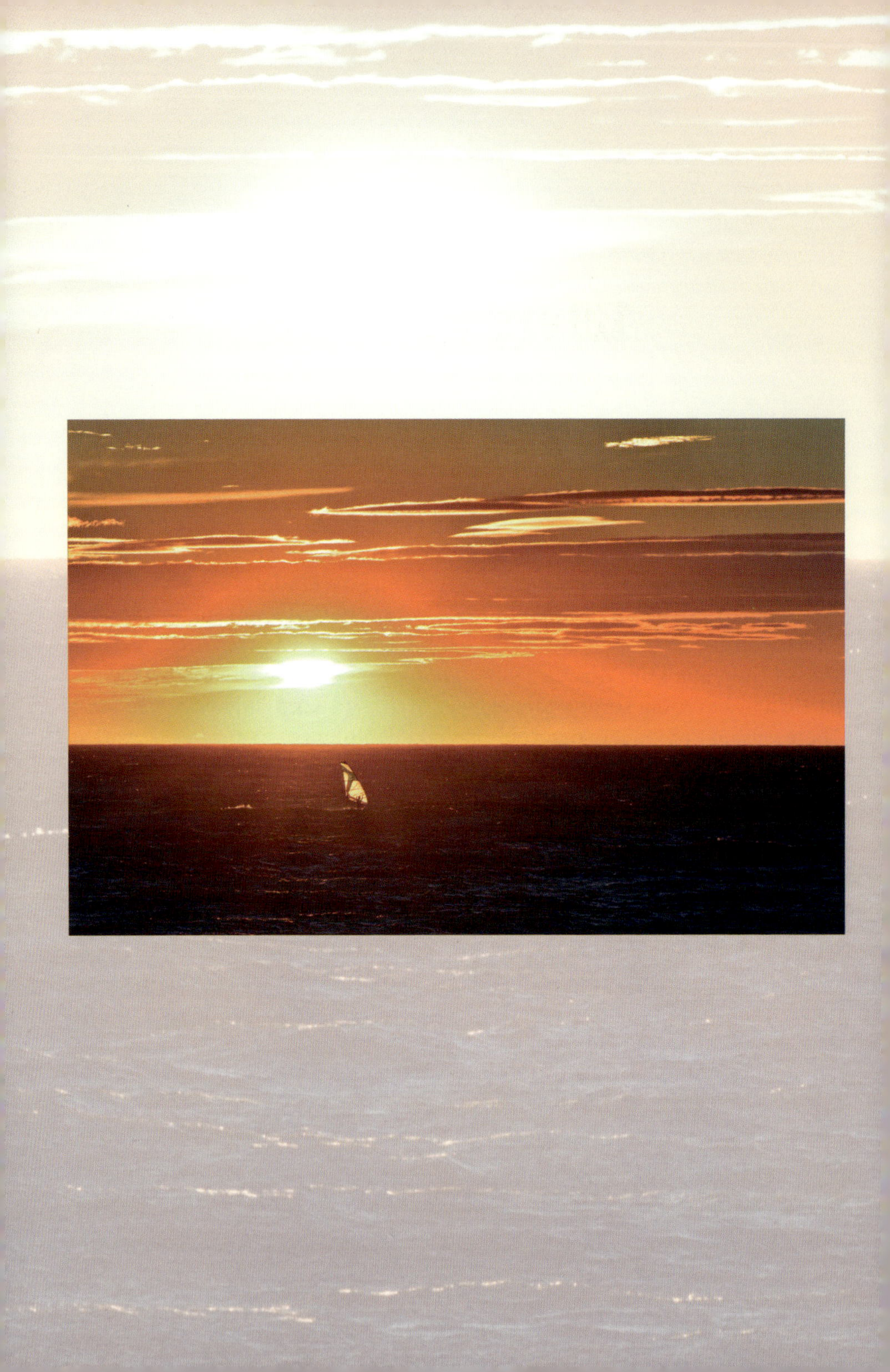

Acts of Kindness

No sunset is ever the same. Much depends on the clouds. The resplendent colour of sunsets inspires awe. Often, when anticipating a magnificent experience, I have been disappointed when dark clouds have suddenly intervened. I find sunsets difficult to predict. Sometimes it is possible to get a good silhouette; this can be a worthwhile compositional challenge. On this particularly evening some years ago on Walney Island, Barrow, I was lucky. There was no immediate foreground to add depth to the picture, but I noticed this solitary windsurfer approaching from my left, so I waited until he was conveniently slipping by in front of the setting sun. I silently thanked him for his kindness, of which he was unaware.

In our lives, that may often be the case. We can be a blessing for someone through a smile, word or gesture, and we'll perhaps never know the good we have done. Of course, we don't reach out in kindness in order to be recognised. Occasionally, someone may let us know how we helped them without our being aware of it. It comes as a surprise. Jesus told us that an act of kindness done to others is done to him, which adds a further dimension to our lives. Others have brightened up our lives too, unawares. Let's thank God today for anonymous 'windsurfers'.

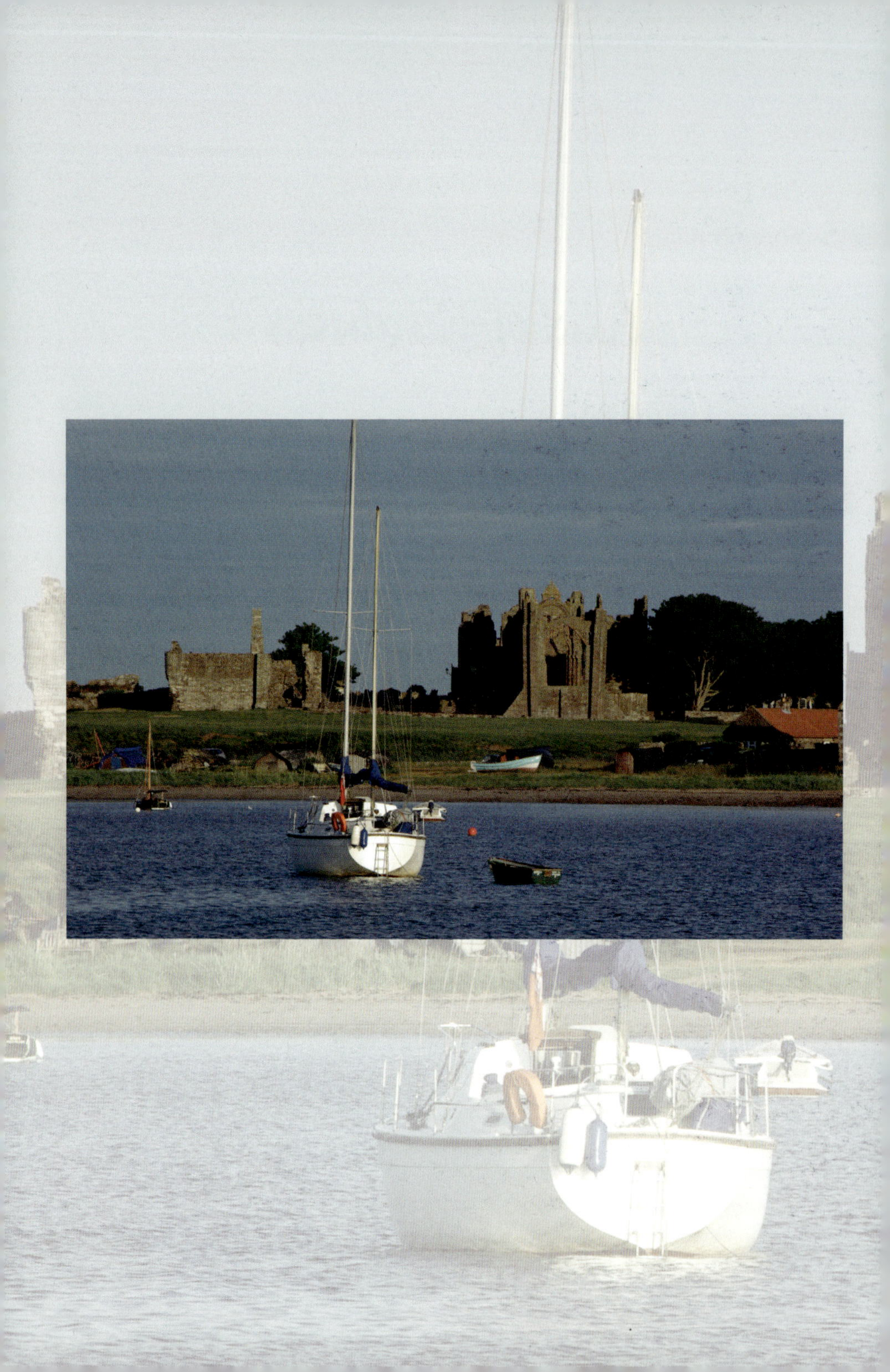

Lasting Legacies

One of my favourite places in the UK is Lindisfarne, also known as Holy Island; it is a tidal island in Northumberland, south of Berwick. I've journeyed there many times, and have occasionally been able to stay overnight with small retreat groups too. This photo captures several aspects of that experience. The harbour is fascinating. Alongside the yachts, there are numerous small fishing boats; fishing is an important part of local life and has been for many centuries. Some of the upturned old wooden boats are used as storage sheds, visible near the water's edge. The sense of community on the island is strong. At the heart of the island is the old monastic abbey, reminding the visitor of the times of the great Celtic Christian missionaries, Aidan and Cuthbert. Here was the cradle of early Celtic Christianity. The monastery was founded in 634. The later abbey was suppressed by Henry VIII in 1536. When the many day visitors have left, Lindisfarne is a haven of peace. It remains a sacred place.

Perhaps today we could pause in appreciation for those men and women to whom we owe so much for their faith, genuine goodness and compassion, and their courageous missionary outreach. Their legacy lingers still; we stand on their shoulders. What will we bequeath to those who come after us?

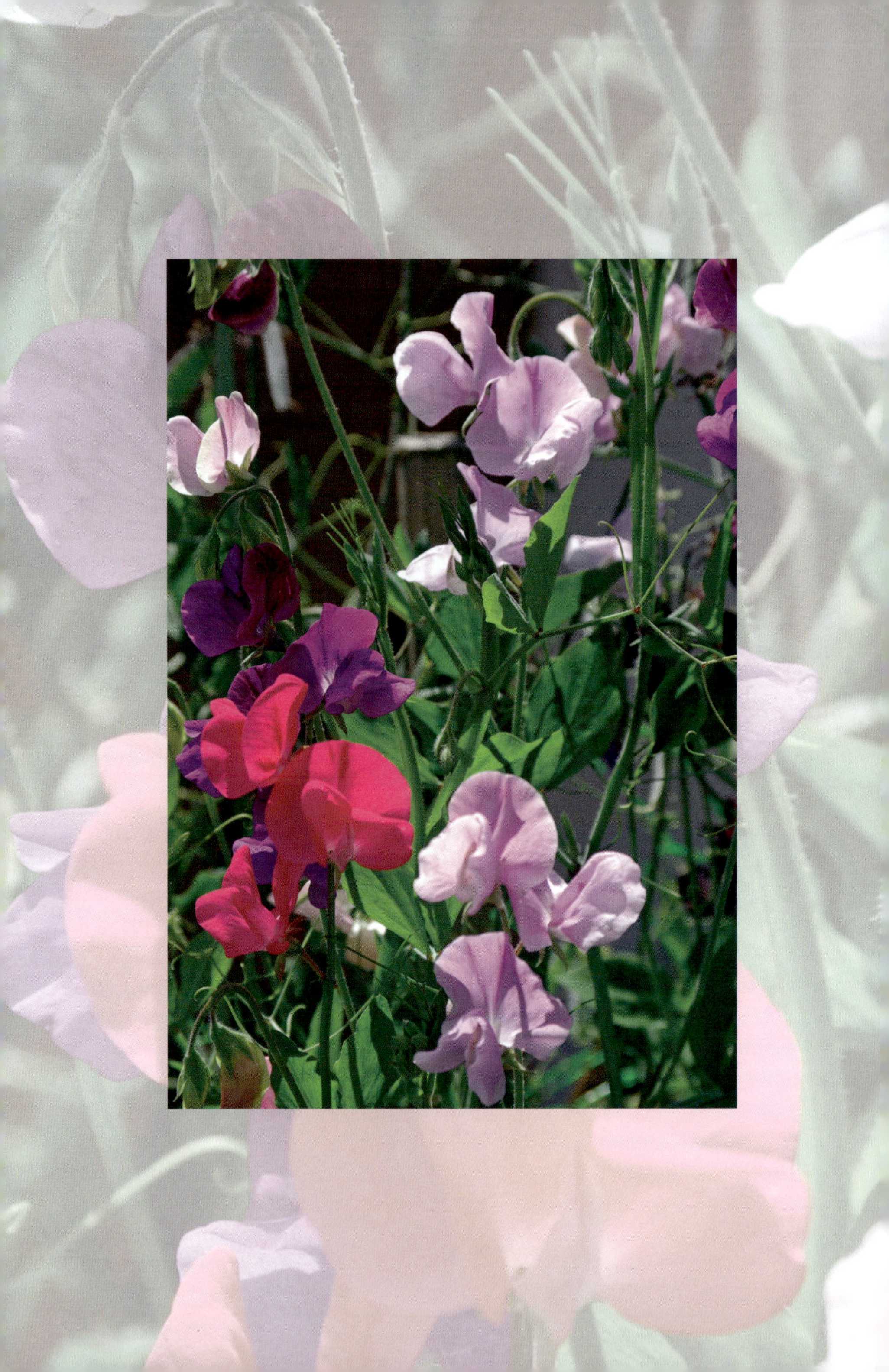

Remembering

Amongst the flowers in the garden at Thornleigh, Bolton, my community residence, two varieties recall the late Br Donald: sunflowers and sweet peas. Donald was a great fan of both, and spent much time and effort to ensure their presence. Swathes of sunflowers are very appealing, but individual specimens never fill me with delight, possibly because they grow too high and tower over me! But I do appreciate the gentle shades and scent of sweet peas.

Since I took this photo, the much loved Br Donald has passed away. Now, whenever I see a sunflower or a group of sweet peas, I call him to mind, thanking God for his life, inspiration and friendship. Have you a favourite flower? Are there flowers which evoke a special person, event or experience for you?

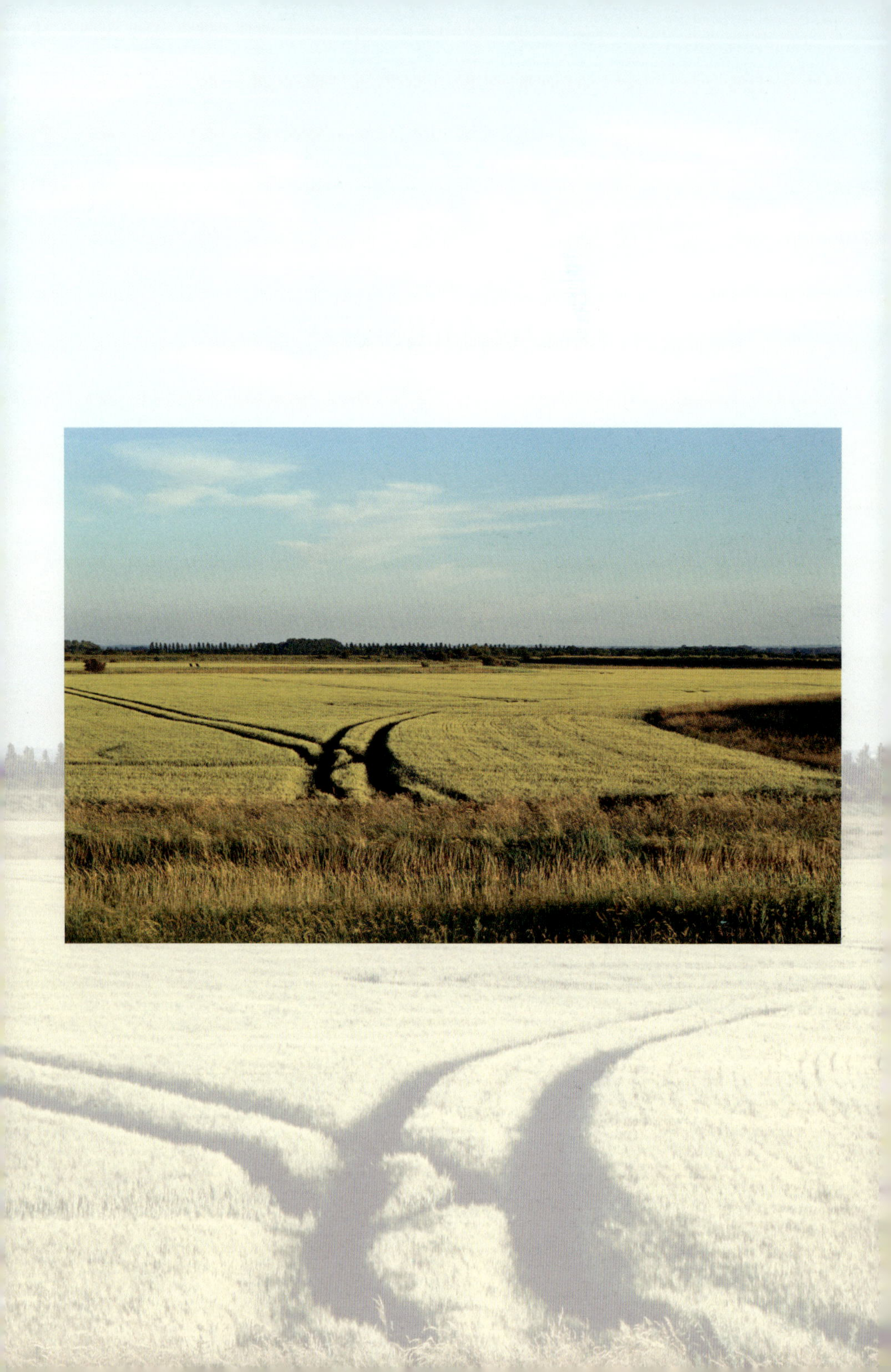

Decisions

I took this photo some years ago in Kent, near Herne Bay. The sea was a few yards behind me! I find it thought-provoking. Decisions! Do I take the left fork, or the right? Whichever path I choose, do I know where it is going? How do I decide between the alternatives? Some decisions are not too difficult or do not have major implications. Others can be lifechanging: the choice of a life partner; a career; a university course or college; a political stance; a faith threshold to cross… Sometimes, we have to make snap decisions; on other occasions, careful discernment is advisable.

Whatever decisions we have to make today, let's not be afraid to involve God's Spirit in the process. As well as helping me make decisions, the Spirit is very good at sorting out the mess when I make the wrong one without Spirit help! Perhaps we could also be more reflective in our ordinary decision making, and not thoughtlessly rush in or do what we always do. This could apply to our driving, our shopping, our use of social media, our conversations, our praying.

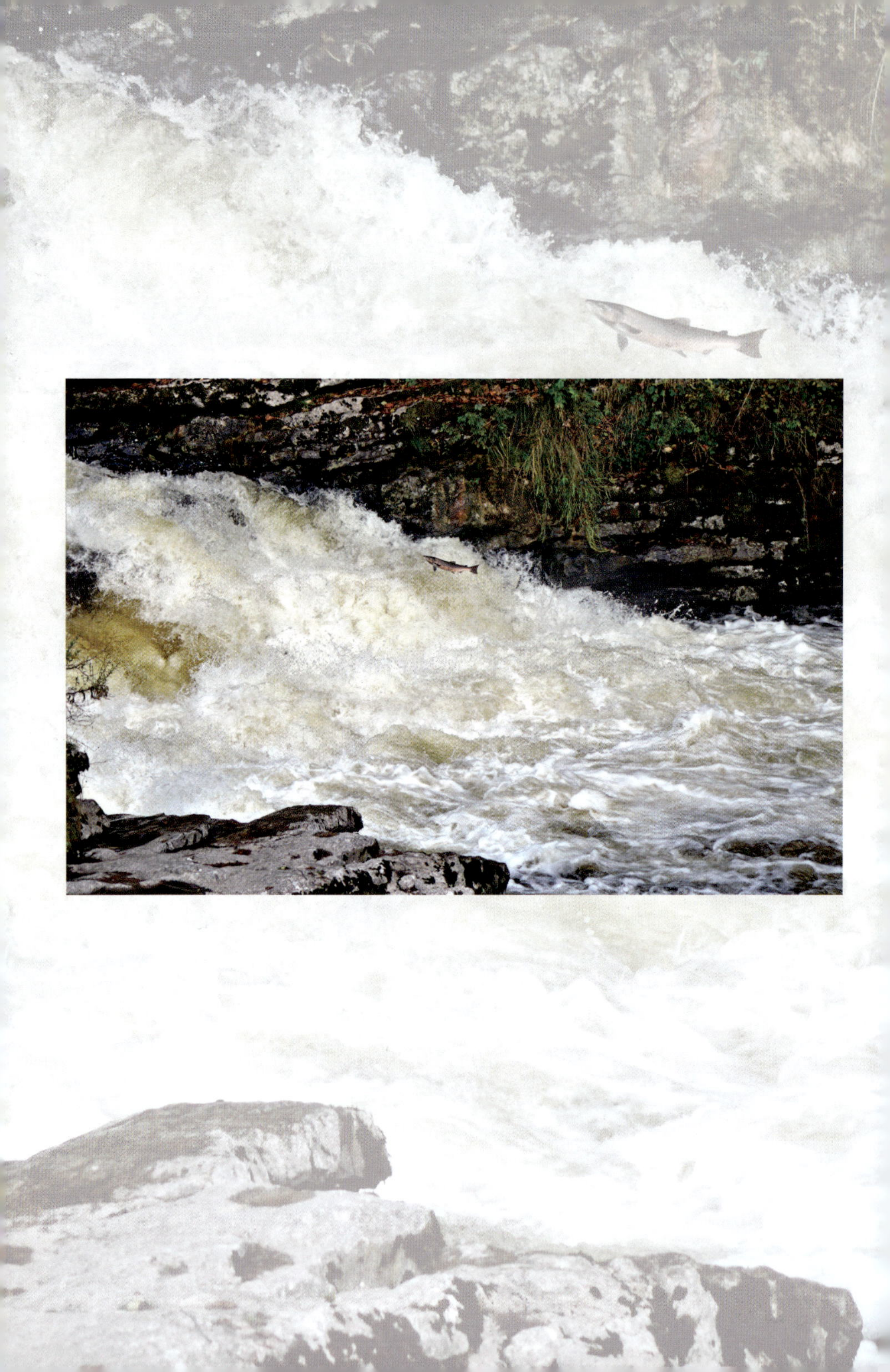

Perseverance

As a child, I used to accompany my dad on fishing expeditions to the local canal. I found it absolutely boring, and quickly reverted to football in the street with my pals. In later life, however, I managed to catch a salmon, with a high shutter speed rather than a rod! This adventure took place on the River Kent, near Brettargh Holt, where the Salesian Sisters used to have a retreat centre. In the early autumn the salmon return to the upper reaches of the river to spawn but are obliged to negotiate the 'salmon leap': not an easy task. I watched them attempting this feat for quite a while, admiring their tenacity and perseverance. The photo catches the challenge they face.

The salmon can, I believe, teach us a salutary lesson. For most achievements in life, effort is needed. To make some dreams come true, we need 'stickability'; obstacles exist in order to be overcome, and this demands courage in the face of failure and disappointment, and requires that we 'try, try and try again'. They say that today's culture is an 'instant' culture, and not only with regard to coffee. This means that the salmon is unlikely to be a mascot or model for many. It also means that there will be much disillusionment around. Let's pray today that we don't become people who give up easily, but people who can 'hang in there' and keep trying. And let's not only pray for 'stickability' but seek to develop it.

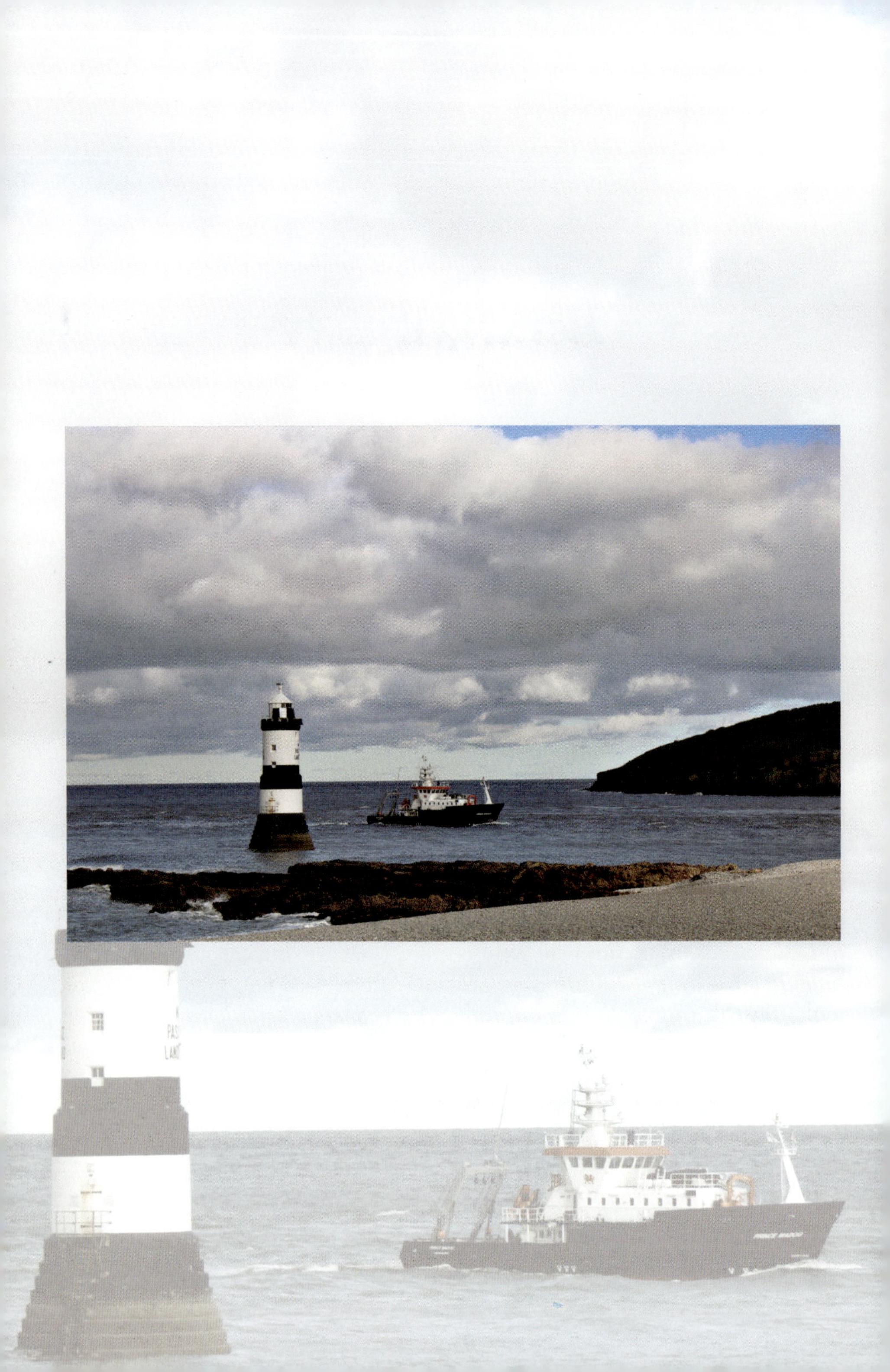

Watchful Care

This is a photo of Trwyn Lighthouse, at Penmon Point, near Beaumaris on the Isle of Anglesey. It was built in 1838 after a ship from Liverpool foundered on the nearby rocks. Looking across at Puffin Island, it guards the entrance to the Menai strait. Like many lighthouses around the country, photographers find this one an interesting subject. I was lucky in that a fishing boat obligingly passed by whilst I was there. Often, lighthouses are situated in challenging terrain, their construction a great achievement.

The main purpose of a lighthouse, obviously, is to warn of danger, and so to prevent shipwrecks and save lives. As we all know, the sea can be an unfriendly and merciless environment. It isn't difficult to switch the imagery and reflect that, as human beings, we can have a similar role. Parents, educators, pastors, friends can be sources of security and safety, can point out potential dangers and threats, can prevent mistakes and misfortunes, and can in this way maintain and enrich the quality of life. Let's reflect on and recommit to our lighthouse role today.

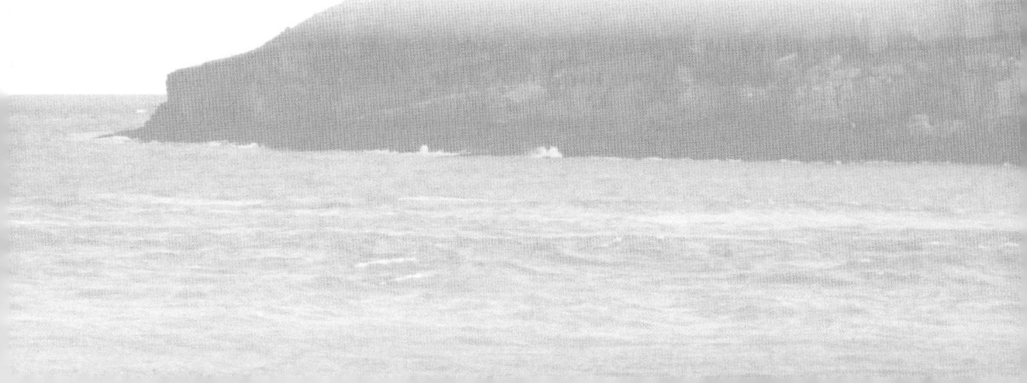

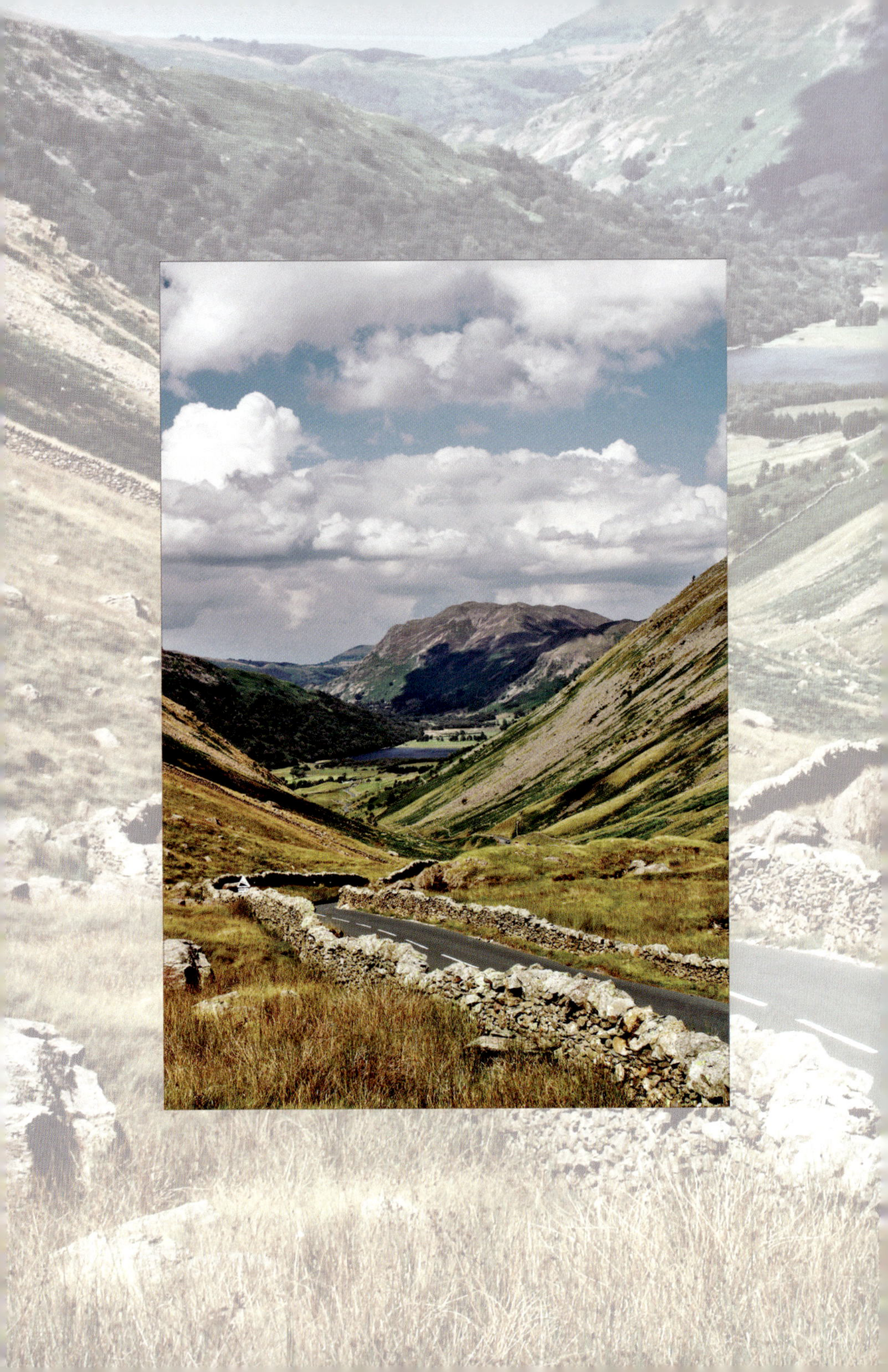

Value the Past

In the Lake District, there are several spectacular mountain passes, which are former routes for transporting goods by horse or mule. Nowadays, the roads tend to be narrow and challenging for the driver of a motorised vehicle. My favourite pass is this one, the Kirkstone, which links the town of Ambleside with Patterdale village and Ullswater lake. This photo was taken from a small carpark on the descent, after the Kirkstone Inn, which stands proudly at 1489 feet, the third highest pub in England. The name 'Kirkstone' comes from a prominent rock which resembles a church steeple; 'kirk' is word for a church in Old English and also in Scotland. Looking down the twisty road of the pass, one catches sight of the small lake of Brotherswater, and beyond rises Place Fell, which, once conquered, offers breathtaking views.

I'm always amazed at the stone walls which are found throughout the Lake District, frequently in places which seem almost inaccessible. I often wonder how long it took to build them, and admire the enormous effort, perseverance and skill which went into their construction. Dry stone walling is a dying art, I'm told. These walls are a boon for landscape photography, moreso than the more recent wooden posts and wire fencing, more easily erected but less attractive. Progress seems to bring great gains, but also entails some loss. Whilst it is good to appreciate the gains, it is important not to forget what has been lost, and the values enshrined in that past.

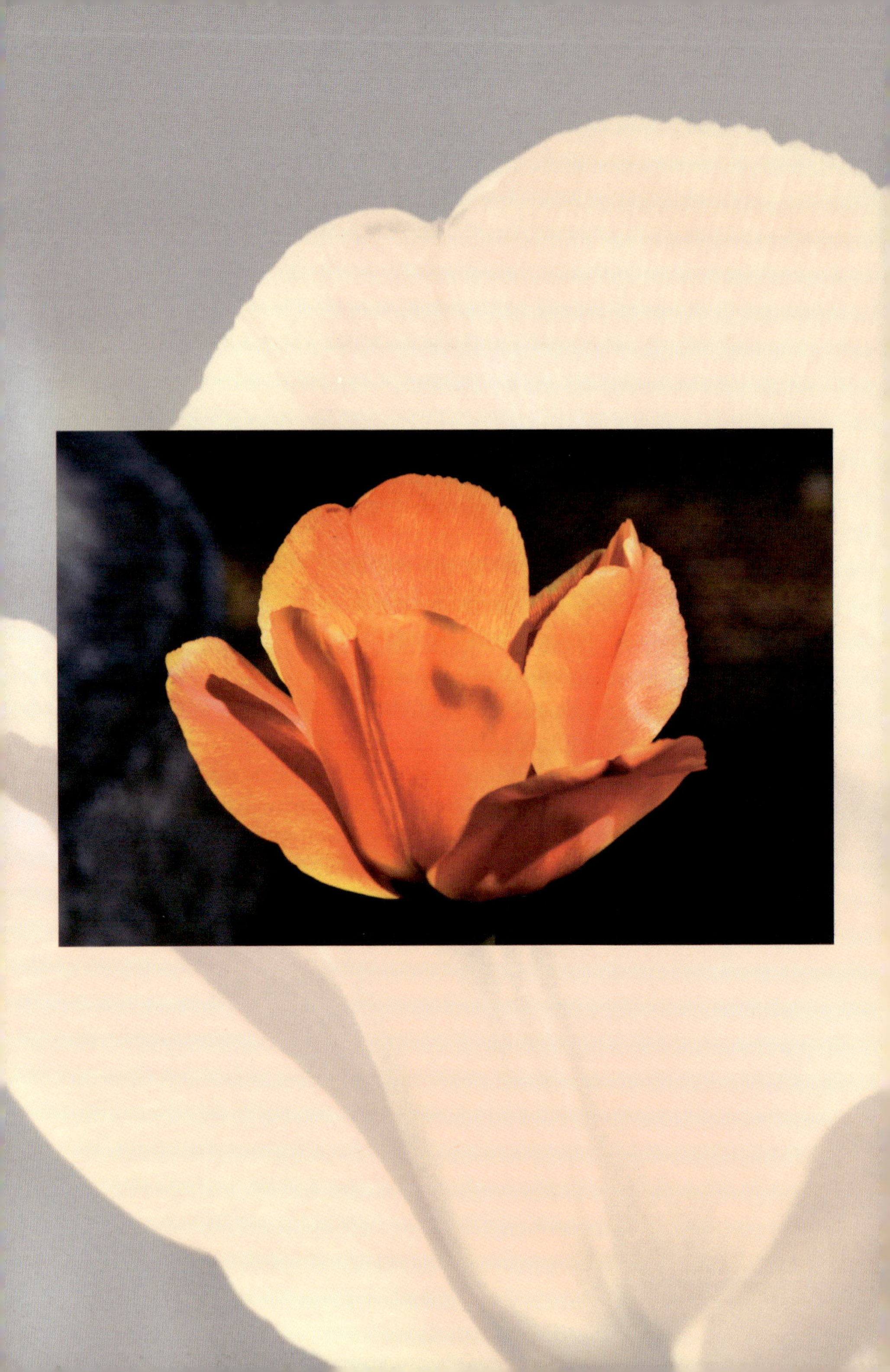

Warmth and Friendship

I love the yellow, orange and russet tints of autumn. The tulip is not an autumn flower, I know, but this flower caught my eye in early spring because of its colour and brightness. This russet colour range is my favourite. When I first had the opportunity to choose curtains for my office and room, these tints featured strongly, and I have always wanted this colour for the car of our Salesian fleet that I was able to use—an unfulfilled desire! I could gaze at this flower all day (or almost!). The way in which the shades merge is fascinating, the play of light and shade is so delicate.

Most of all, this colour speaks to me of warmth. And warmth is such a beautiful human characteristic. Some people exude warmth naturally; a reassuring smile, cheery word or gesture is shown effortlessly. Warmth is an expression of acceptance, it offers encouragement, conveys a sense of belonging, it brightens and transforms people's lives. Try to bring some warmth to others today. If you are not naturally a warm person, why not try to find ways of developing that characteristic?

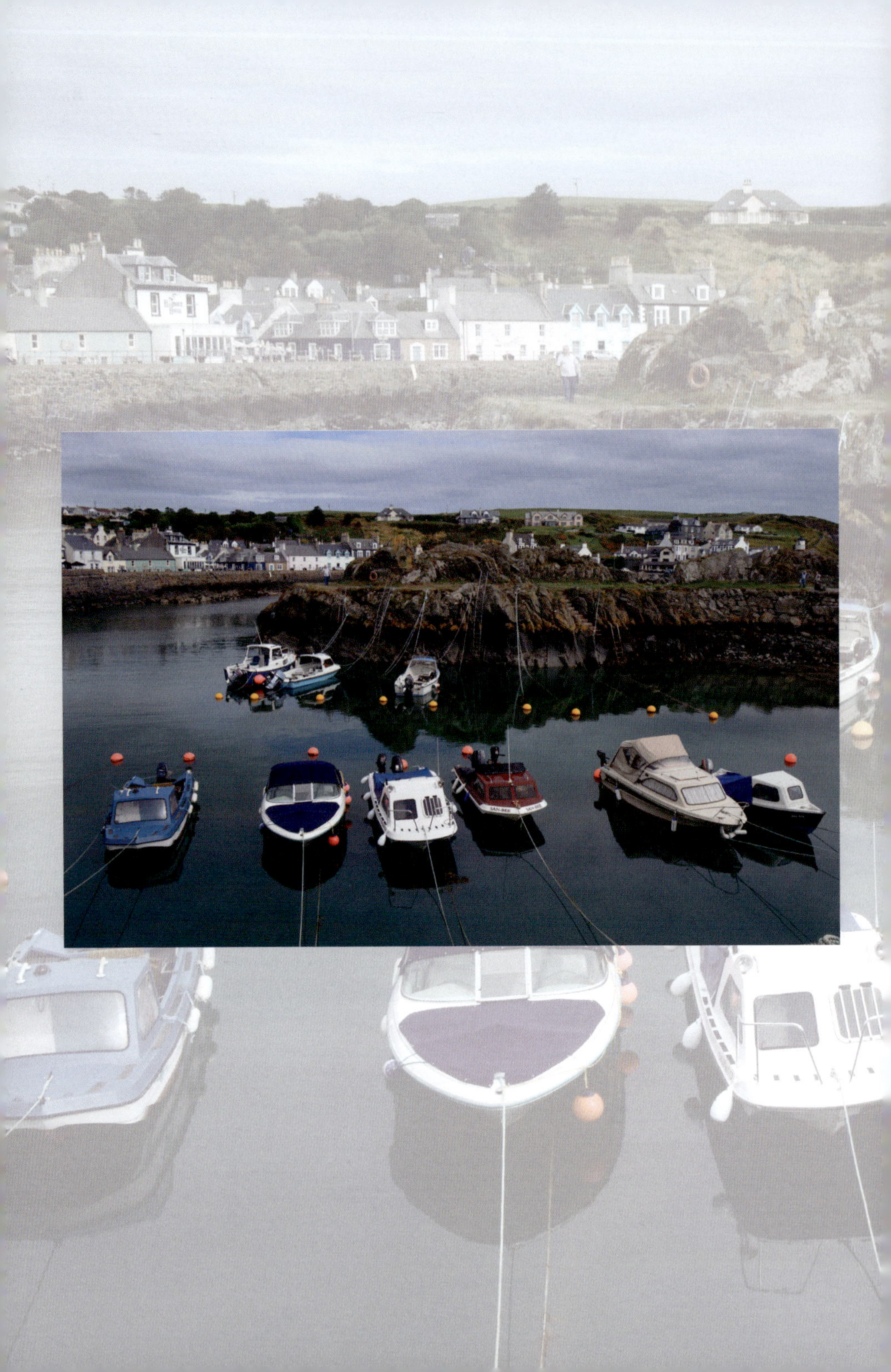

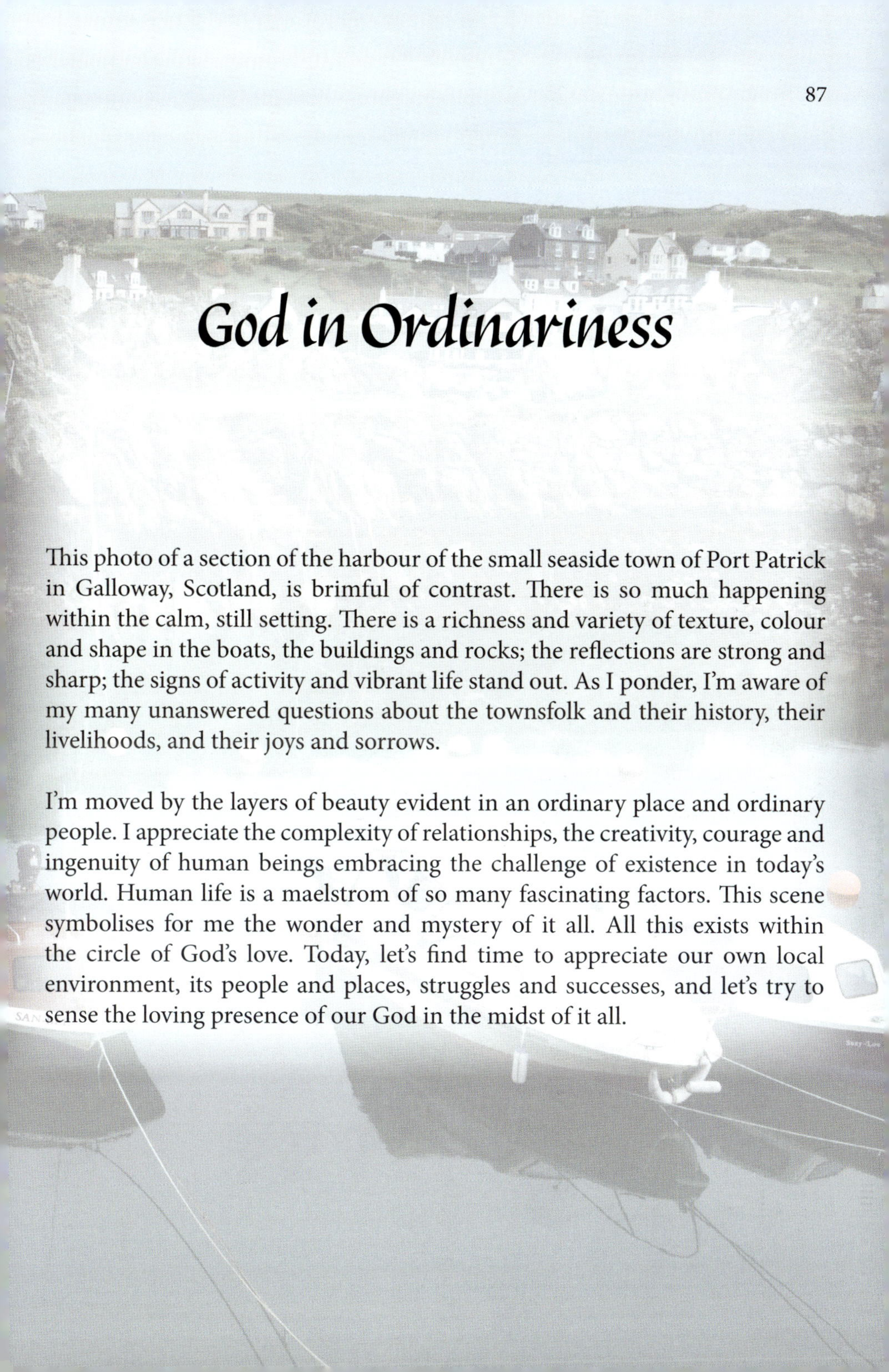

God in Ordinariness

This photo of a section of the harbour of the small seaside town of Port Patrick in Galloway, Scotland, is brimful of contrast. There is so much happening within the calm, still setting. There is a richness and variety of texture, colour and shape in the boats, the buildings and rocks; the reflections are strong and sharp; the signs of activity and vibrant life stand out. As I ponder, I'm aware of my many unanswered questions about the townsfolk and their history, their livelihoods, and their joys and sorrows.

I'm moved by the layers of beauty evident in an ordinary place and ordinary people. I appreciate the complexity of relationships, the creativity, courage and ingenuity of human beings embracing the challenge of existence in today's world. Human life is a maelstrom of so many fascinating factors. This scene symbolises for me the wonder and mystery of it all. All this exists within the circle of God's love. Today, let's find time to appreciate our own local environment, its people and places, struggles and successes, and let's try to sense the loving presence of our God in the midst of it all.

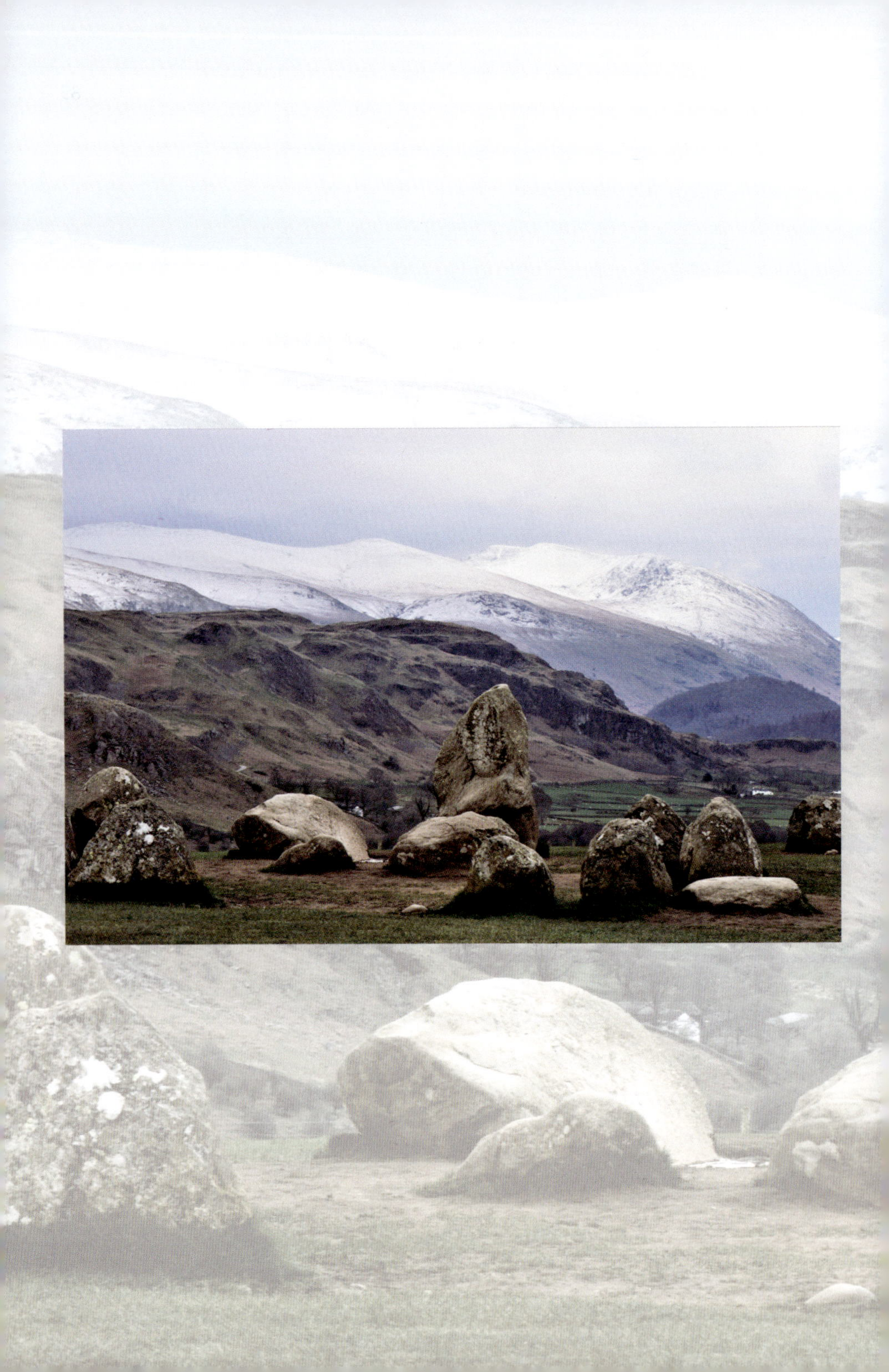

Places of Prayer

This is a winter photo of Castlerigg stone circle near Keswick in the Lake District. I remember that the day I visited this place was extremely windy and numbingly cold; photography wasn't easy. The circle is thought to date back to around 3500 BCE, the Neolithic period, and is considered to be one of the earliest circles in the country. It has been stated that this circle is perhaps the most atmospheric and dramatically sited circle in Britain. The snow-covered Helvellyn massif as background supports that claim. Originally, there were forty-two stones; now there are thirty-eight.

Stone circles like this were important meeting places for the people of the locality, and were used for trading purposes and for prayer and worship. What a spectacular place for liturgy and prayer! They are perhaps the forerunners of magnificent cathedrals like Durham and York. It is possible to pray anywhere, for God is always with us, but some of us have a favourite place. Have you a special place where you prefer to pray?

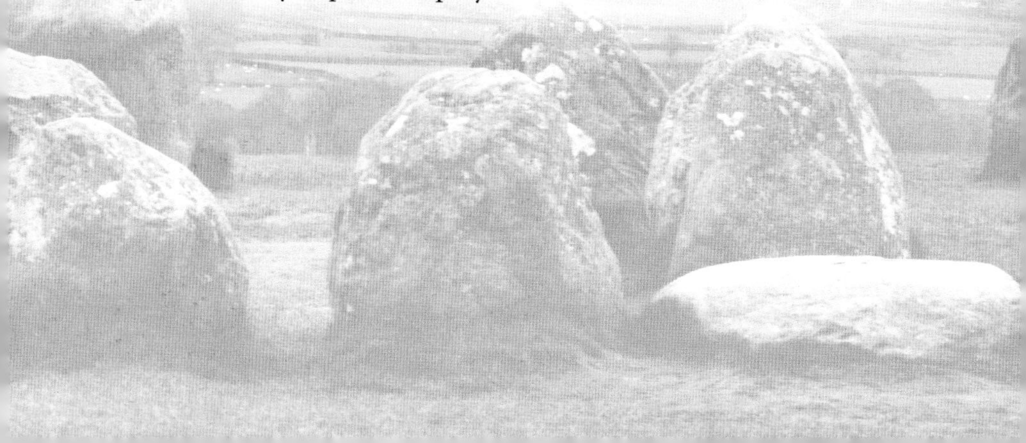

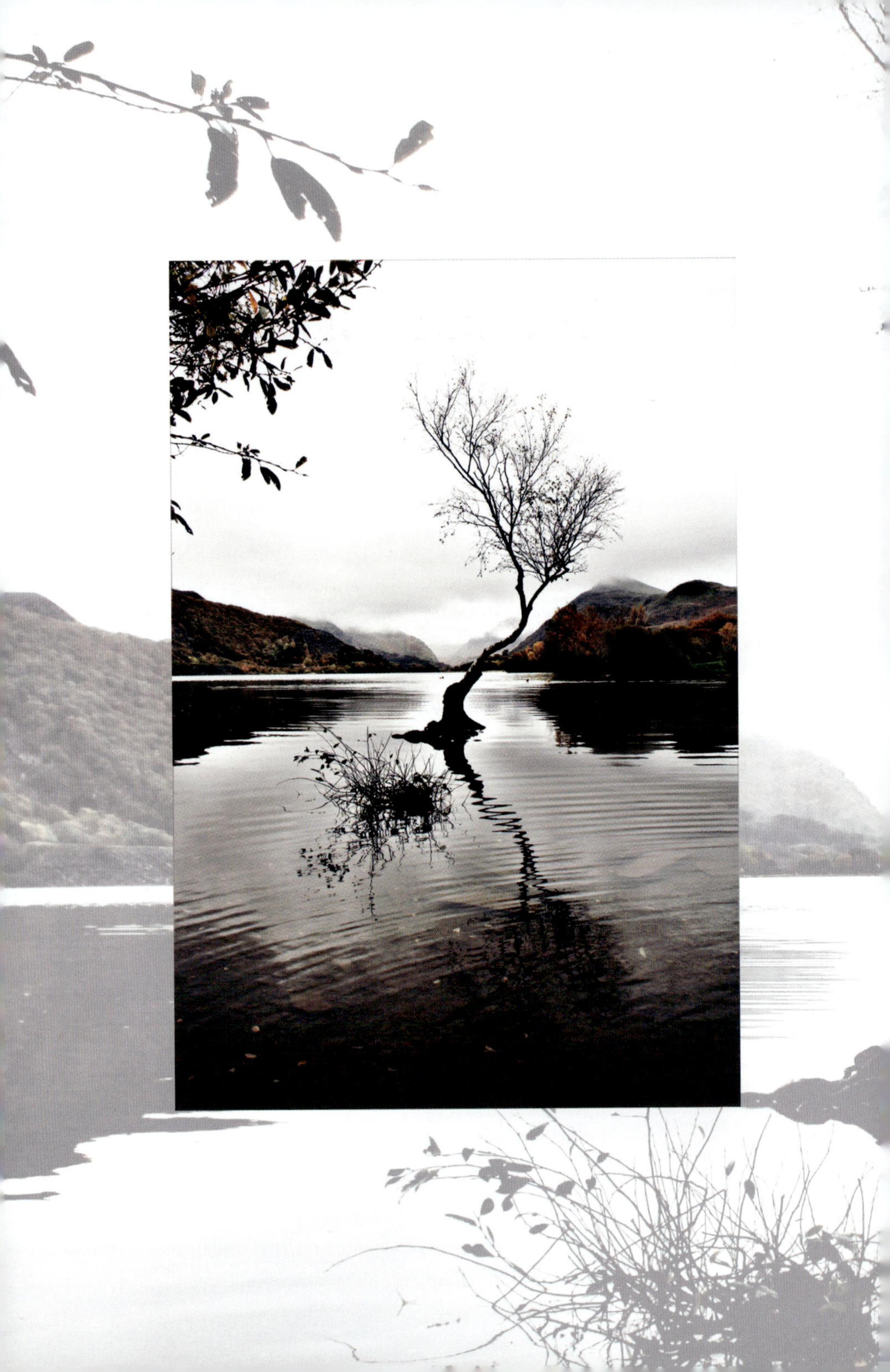

Reminiscing

In an earlier reflection, we thought about lone trees. The lone tree above is to be found in North Wales on the outskirts of Llanberis village at the heart of Snowdonia (Eryri). The Llyn is named Padarn. I managed to find the tree at the second attempt, having spent some time the previous day at the wrong end of the lake! Apparently, this tree is a 'must have' for landscape photographers, though it now has one branch fewer than in most of the photos I've seen. It isn't difficult to be captivated by its simple charm, especially with autumn tints around, and reflections, and the distant mist shrouding the Snowdonia massif. I have a copy of this picture on the wall in my room. It recalls a special place, a special experience.

What are the pictures which adorn the walls where you live and work? How significant are they? Perhaps today could be an occasion for looking at them again more reflectively, and reminiscing.

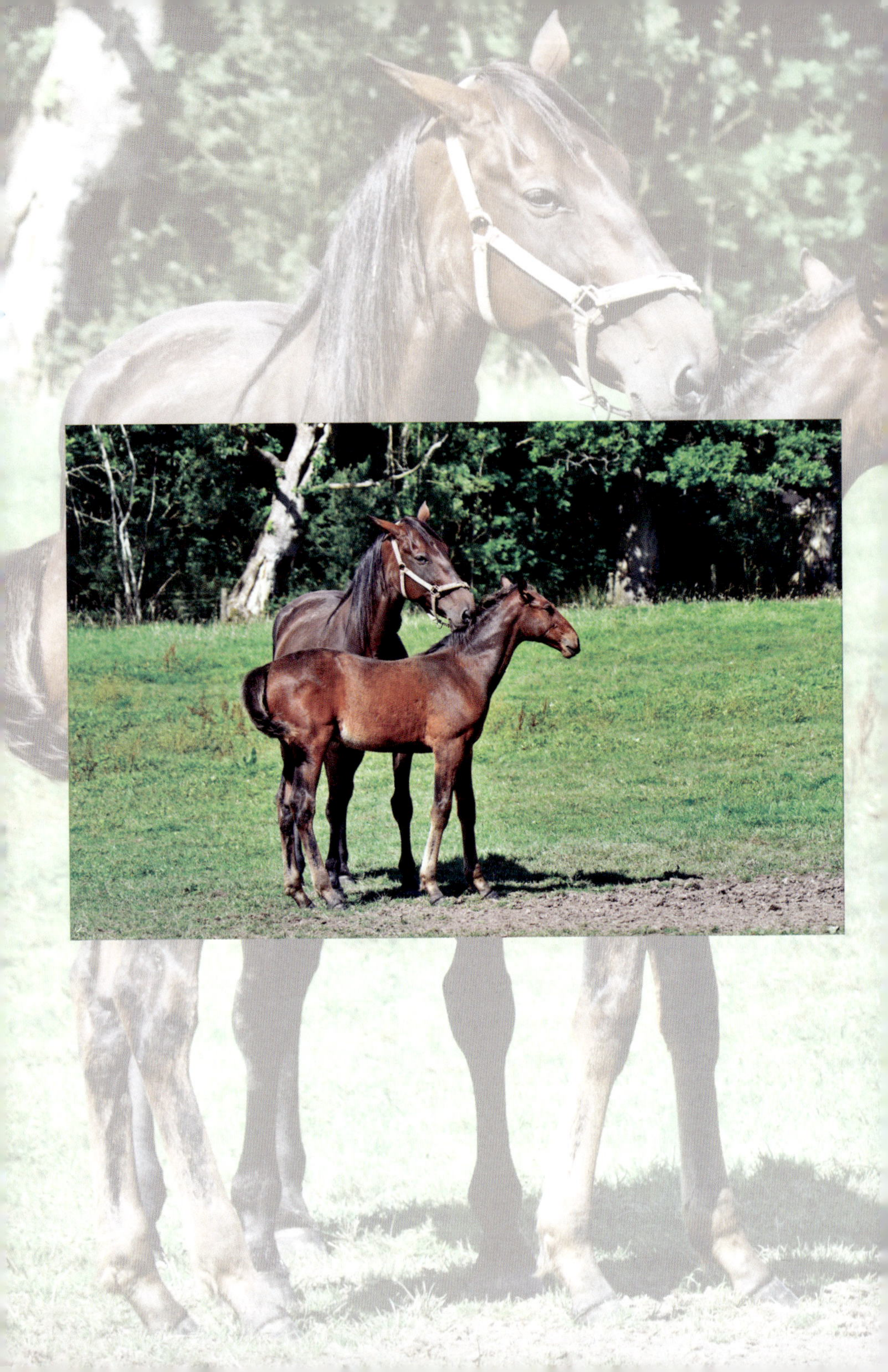

Motherly Love

I often muse about canals. Today's picture was captured whilst I was walking along the canal in Ulverston, built in 1796, which was used for the exporting of slate, copper and linen. Now it is a popular place to take a walk. The sight of mother and child is universally beautiful and moving. There is something wonderful about a mother's care for her offspring, here a mare and foal; in the next field there were cows with calves, sheep with lambs. This, of course, is true for our human experience. The generous, unselfish care of our mother has contributed so much to our becoming who we are; the lack of such care is a great tragedy.

I believe that it is a mother's love which awakens us to the mystery of God's love. A friend of mine prays to God as mother and father, not just father. There are examples in the Old Testament where qualities we usually consider to be feminine are applied to God, like gentleness and compassion. Isaiah, for instance uses nurturing imagery of God: "like a son comforted by his mother will I comfort you." Let's take time today to thank God for our mother, and pray for mothers, especially single mothers, who may be struggling in the current financial climate.

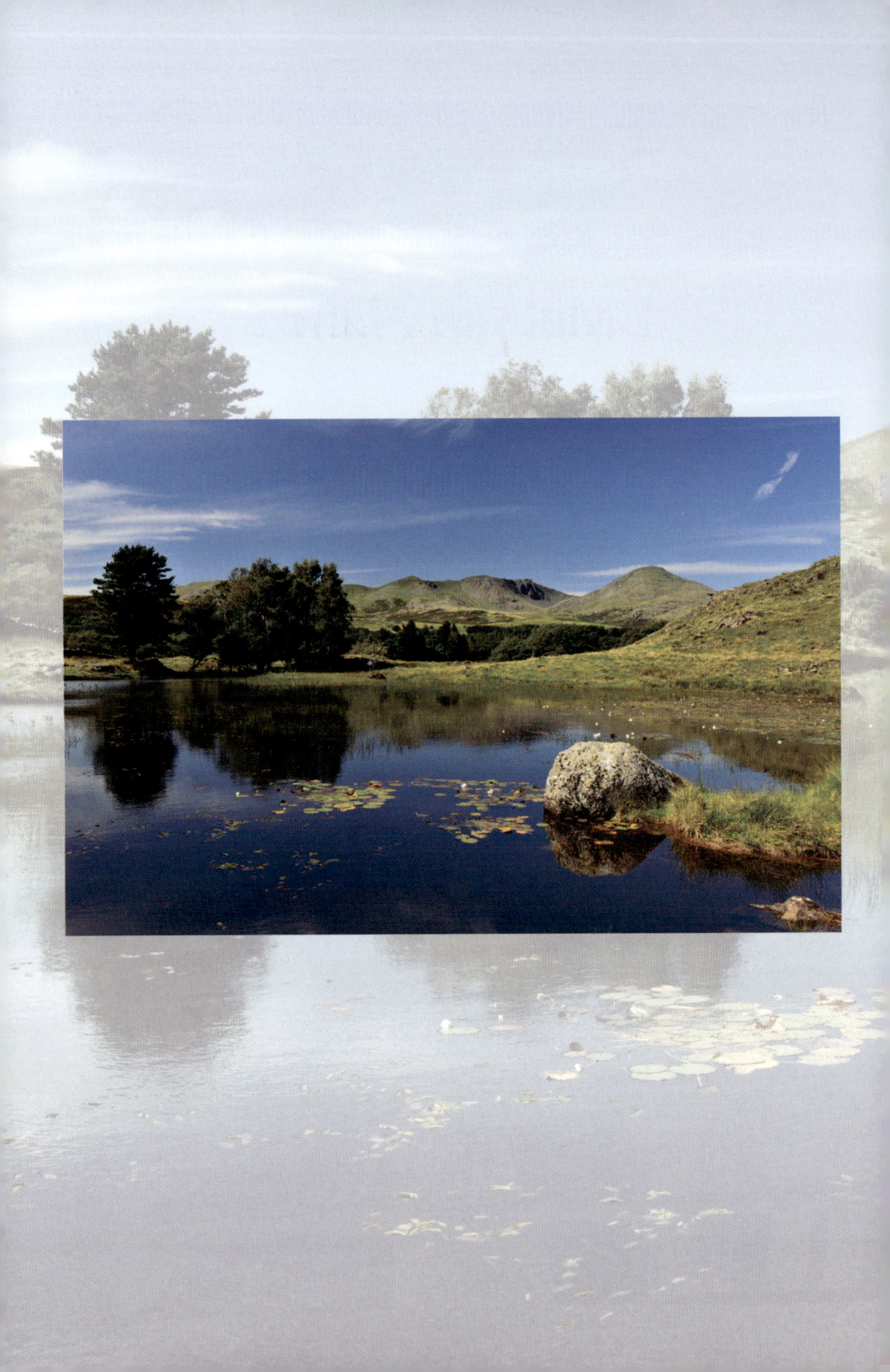

Beauty in Nature

Perhaps we all have our favourite views, wherever we live, wherever we visit. This is certainly one of mine. The Kelly Tarn rock and water lilies in the foreground, the reflections, the Old Man of Coniston and Dow Crag in the background, the variety and clarity of shade and texture, the fine light and plenty of blue in the sky, combine to produce a memorable scene. Sadly, a recent visit revealed that the fine pine tree on the left of the frame is no longer there; it was blown down in one of the storms this year. No one will ever take this picture again!

There is amazing beauty in every land, and here in the UK we have a fair share of it. I believe it is so enriching to value, appreciate and enjoy it, and to thank our God for it. We are truly blessed. Gazing at a beautiful scene or flower can bring peace and healing. At the same time, much of our natural world is precarious and under threat. Climate change is a reality. There are serious threats to our environment. As human beings, we can be thoughtless and destructive. Today, let's make a point of admiring something beautiful, and try to avoid anything detrimental to such beauty.

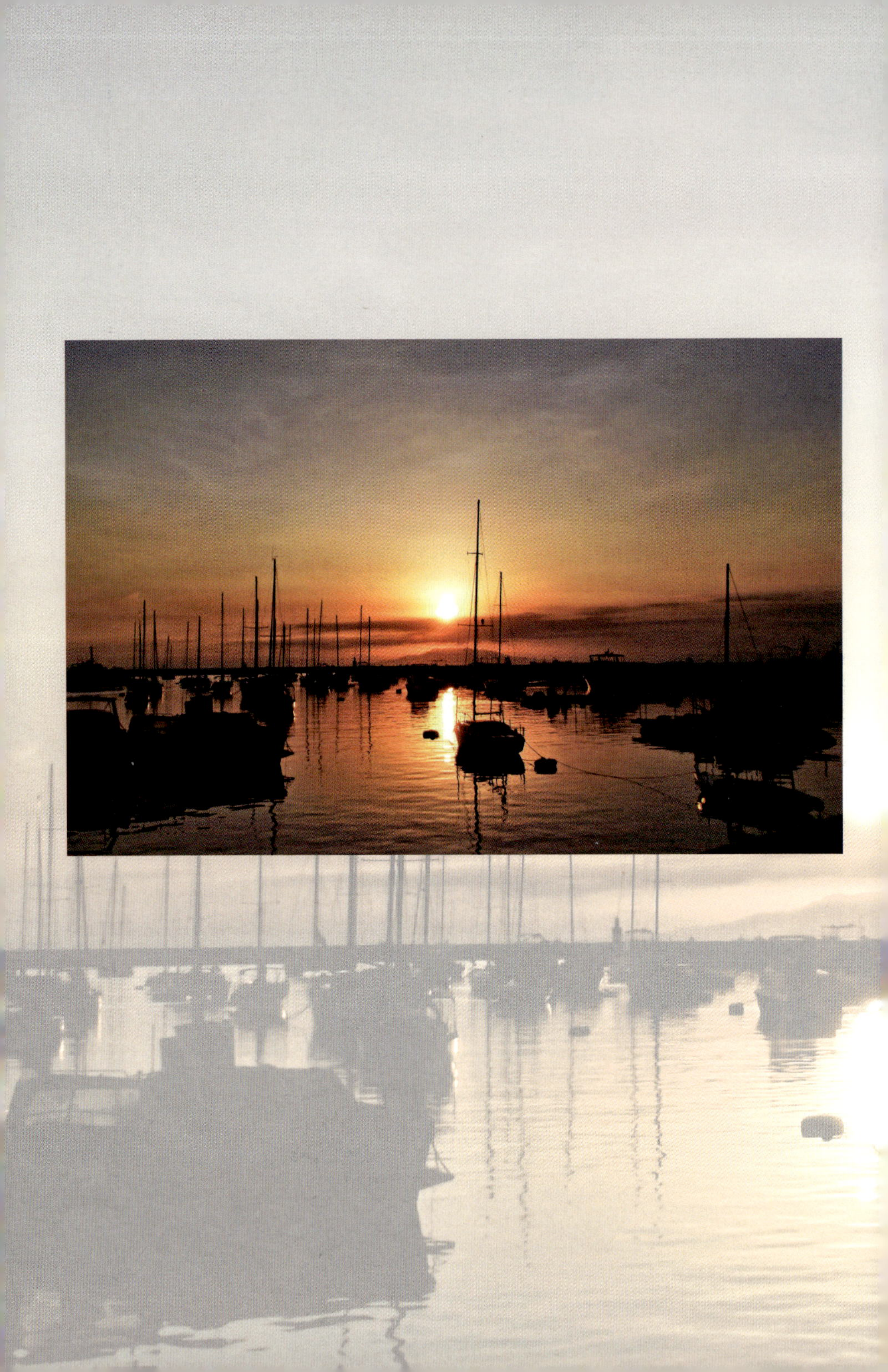

Respect and Reverence

We are again in the Philippines, this time on the coast near Manila. That evening I was hoping for a bright sunset, so frequent over the bay. However, I was happy to accept this more subtle event. Note the bird perched on the mast of the central boat, safe and secure!

In today's world, gentleness, humility and subtle beauty are not common. Communication can be loud, aggressive, harsh, disrespectful. I cringe frequently when listening to our politicians, sports pundits, folk involved in the media generally. People with authority in the Church at times can be uncompromising, lacking in sensitivity, blinkered in their reading of reality. Let's today seek to be gentle in sharing our views and in dealing with others, treating people not only with respect, but with reverence.

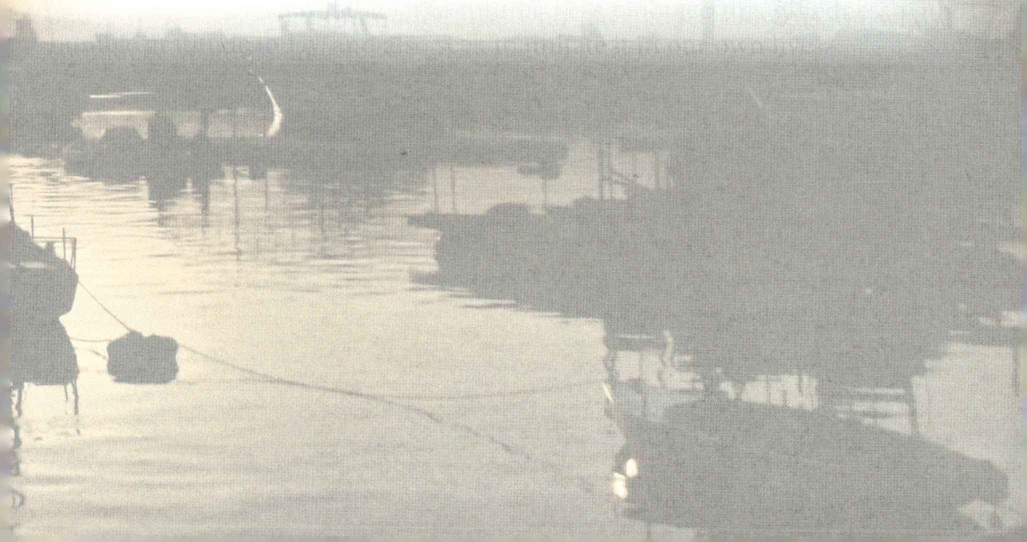

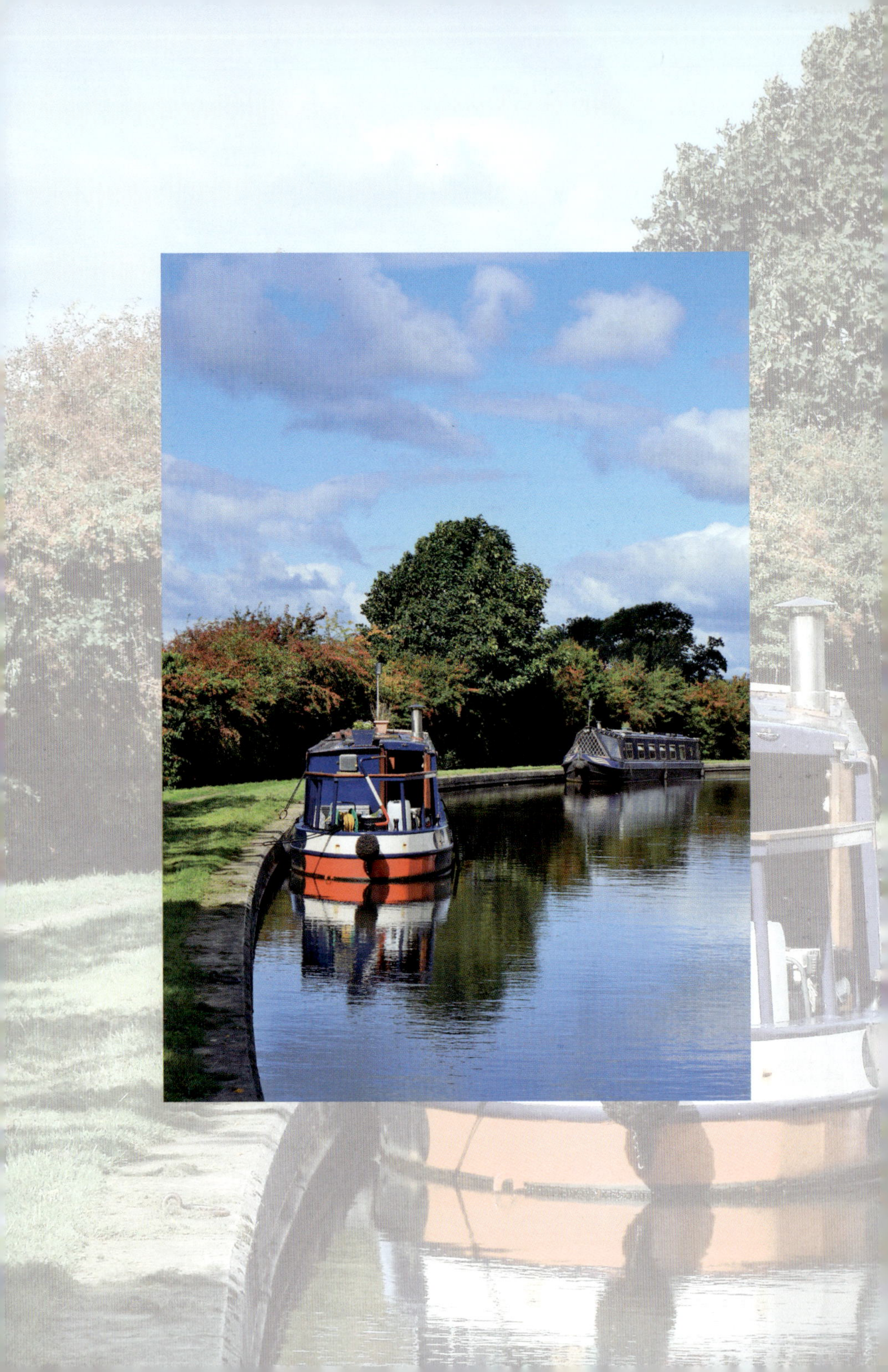

Adapt and Grow

Canals again. This photo was taken near the Galgate Marina on the Lancaster Canal on a bright day in early autumn. The former towpath now provides several miles of good walking with no hills to climb, and some pleasant and varied scenery. Some of the boats are colourful and bright. Swans and ducks are abundant. Usually a public house isn't far away!

The change from industry to pleasure in the use of canals illustrates our human capacity for adaptability. As life becomes faster and technology develops, we have all had to become more adaptable in order to cope. Some find it easier than others, or find it easier to adapt to some things and not to others. I've struggled with having to get a parking app in order to pay at the car park! Our ability to adapt was stretched to the limit in the COVID pandemic. But adaptability is also required in relationships, whether in school, parish, family or workplace. It is demanded when people get old or fall ill. It is then an expression of compassion and care. In having to adapt, we can discover inner qualities we were not aware of before, new levels of invention and creativity. Perhaps today we could ask ourselves how adaptable we really are, and whether we need to grow in this regard.

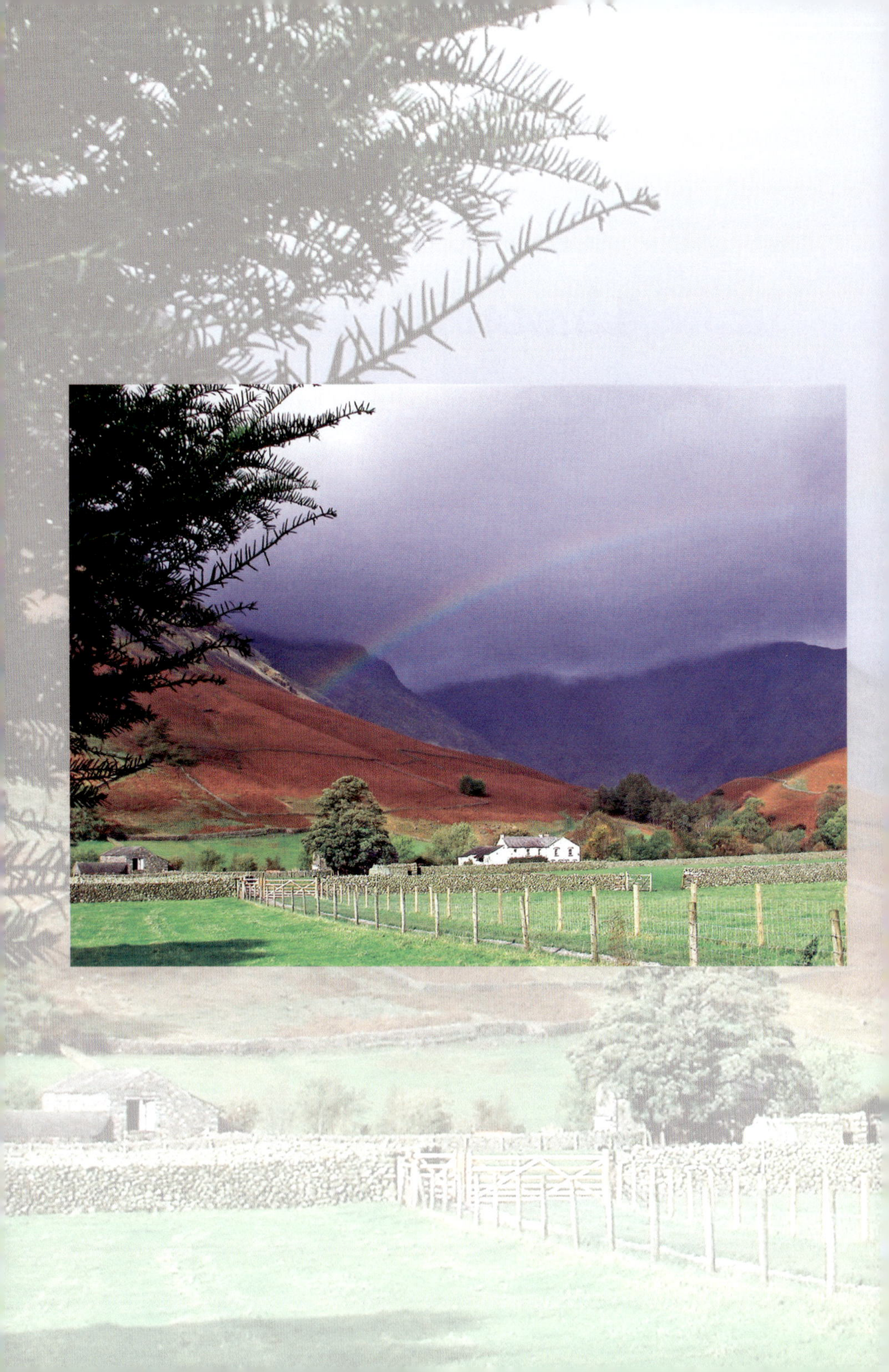

Thank You, God

Autumn is a wonderful time of year; the variety and depth and beauty of the colours can be breathtaking. Wasdale is my favourite Lake District venue, with its brooding lake, disconcerting screes, and the little village of Wasdale Head, which opens up to the mountains. This photo was taken from the modest graveyard next to the chapel of St Olaf, as the fronds of yew might suggest, where several climbers who lost their lives in serious falls are buried, a healthy reminder of the need for care on the fells. The photo has a poignancy for me, for my companion that day was Br Donald MacDonald, who was recovering from a serious operation, a wonderful friend to many of us, who has since gone to God. Following the leading line of the pathway and fence, it's possible to make out the countless stones which form the walls, not only in the foreground, where they tend to be almost round in shape, but on the hillsides too. One can only wonder how long it must have taken to build them, and admire the effort and workmanship involved.

That day, the light was special, highlighting the russet of the ferns, bringing out the contrast with the fading green of the grass and trees, and the stark white of the cottage. And, of course, there is a rainbow, always a source of wonder, and mist over Pillar. Thank you, God.

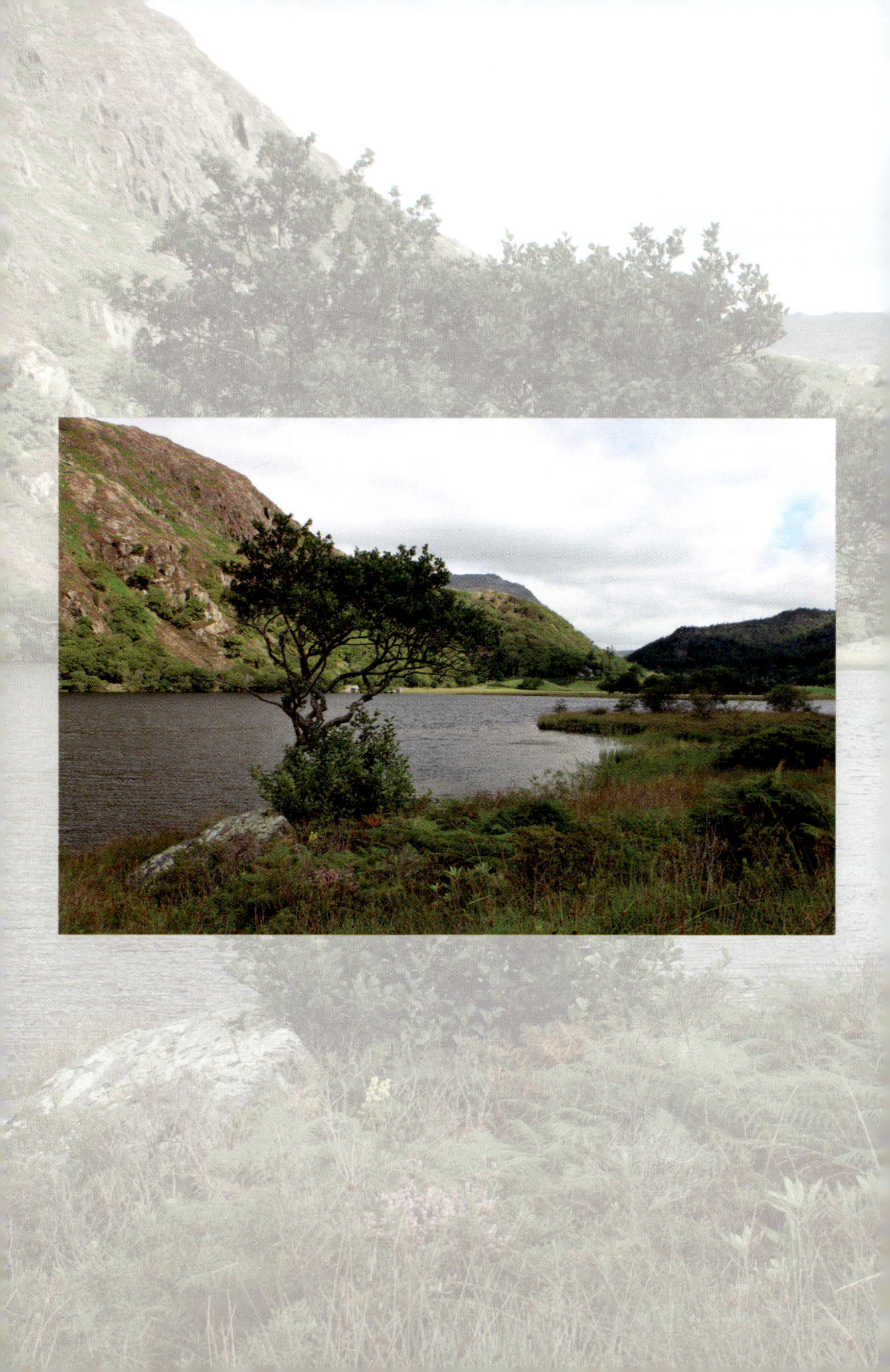

Different Perspectives

Another lone tree, this time at Llyn Dinas in North Wales. I managed to frame a boathouse within its interesting branch formation. It wasn't easy to get near enough. During COVID lockdown, I discovered short YouTube photography videos, and this llyn featured on one of them, so I thought I'd pay a visit next time I was in this area. It's a delightful little stretch of water, a main road on one side, rendering access easy, and a forest and high hills on the other, offering interesting possibilities for hiking. It's an ideal spot for young people to learn canoeing. As I think I commented on an earlier reflection, I am attracted to lone trees, especially if they stand next to water. I like this one because of its branches, and also its setting next to a rock, with heather, flowers and rich vegetation in the foreground. The gap in the hills indicates the route of the nearby road, suggesting journeys and movement. But my eyes constantly return to the tree.

Next time I visit Llyn Dinas, I'd like to take a picture of the tree from the other side, looking down the Llyn in the opposite direction, and get a different perspective. That's an attitude in life which can be creative and enriching.

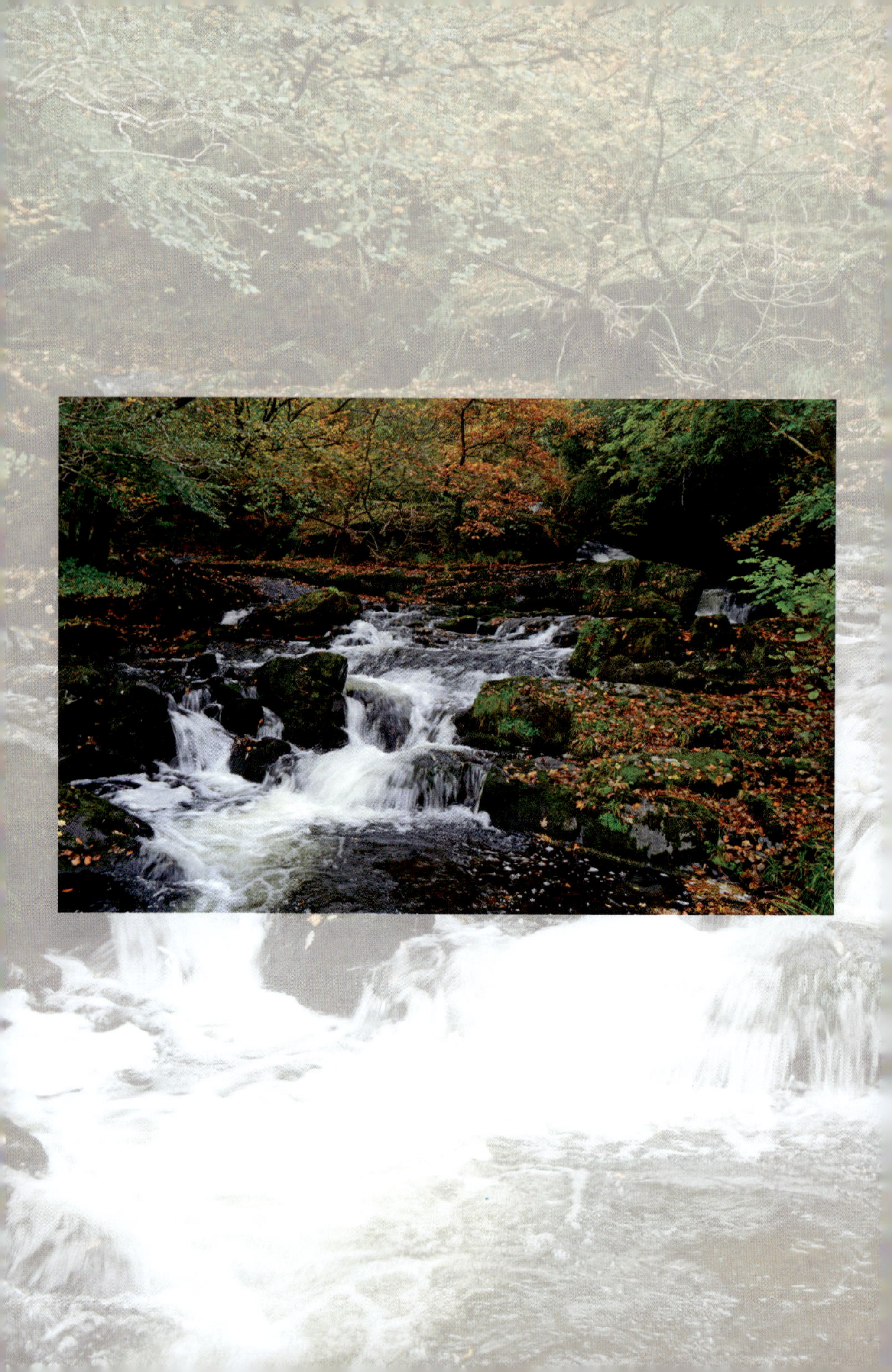

Harmony

I love waterfalls. This interest has developed since I realised that I can no longer manage the high fells. I hadn't realised how many beautiful falls there are in the Lake District, and how fortunate we are. A waterfall is one of the benefits of living in areas where the rainfall can be considerable! Sometimes many ribbons of white decorate the hillsides. In the psalms, we thank God for rivers and seas, fountains and springs, but not for waterfalls. This puzzled me for quite a while, until a learned friend pointed out that there is no word in ancient Hebrew for a waterfall, because there aren't any in Israel! Poor Jesus, he really missed out! This photo catches the beginnings of Force Falls, next to a little village on the country route to Hawkshead. The greens and autumnal russets enhance the image greatly, I think. On another occasion, the falls were in spate, the noise almost deafening. One of the local residents, who had to live with such music, called it 'white noise'.

This photo speaks to me of harmony: harmony in colour and texture; harmony between the static and the moving; and, on that particular occasion, harmony between nature and a human being called Michael. Throughout my life, harmony between people has been an important ideal for me in daily relationships and in ministry. It is so central to the following of Jesus and the meaning of Eucharist. In our discordant world today, the establishing and maintaining of harmony can be a daunting challenge, almost countercultural. Perhaps we can reflect on where we currently stand in our own lives. Do we foster harmony or sometimes introduce disharmony into the lives of others? How can we do more of the first alternative and less of the second?

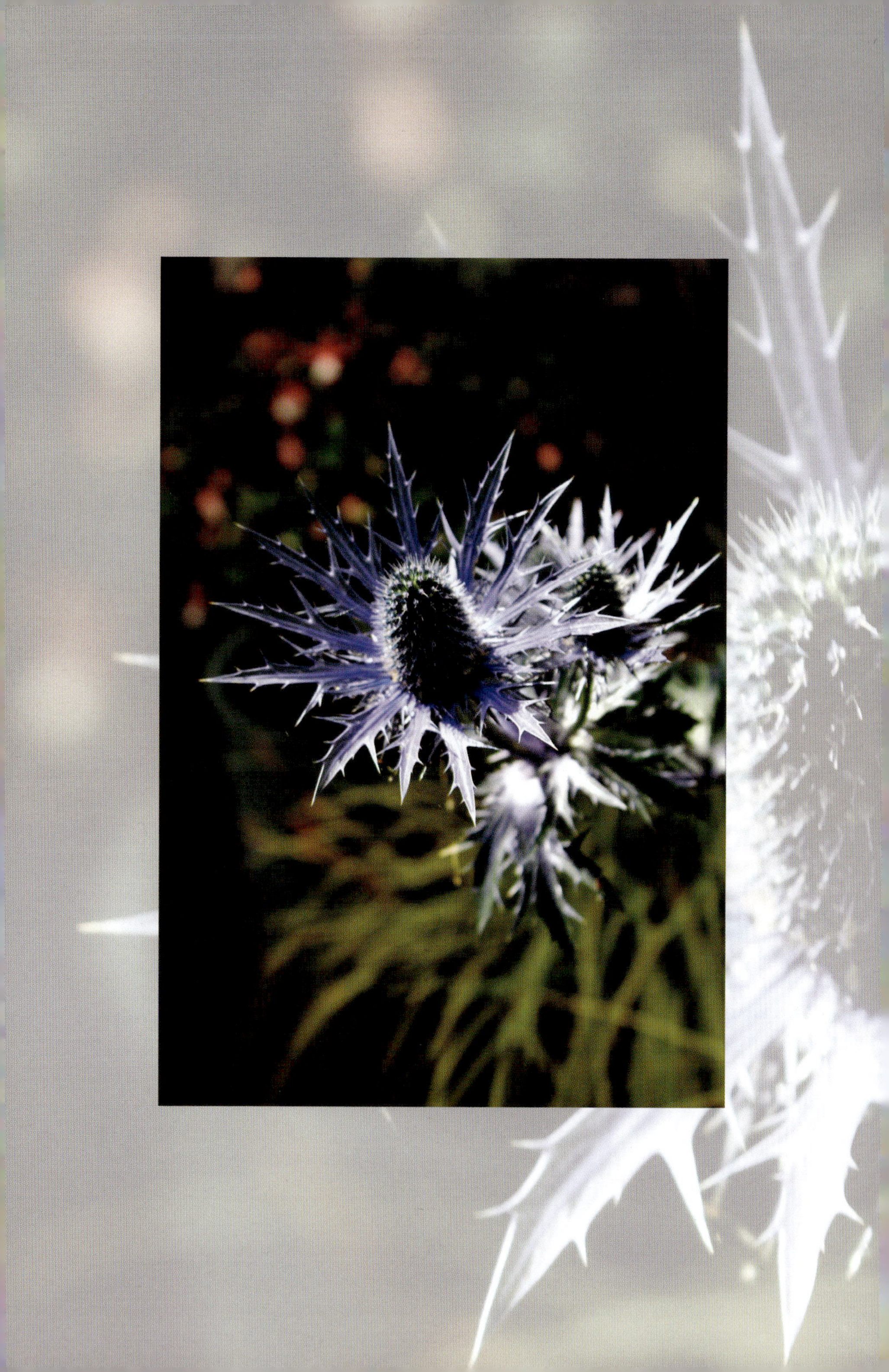

Unexpected Surprises

This is a rather unusual flower which appeared unexpectedly in early summer outside the Publications Office at Thornleigh House. It caught my eye one afternoon as I parked the car. It was the colour which attracted me at first, and then I saw the thorns. On testing them, I realised that they were very sharp and prickly! I believe that this is an Alpine Sea Holly. With a name like that, I cannot understand how it was growing in Bolton!

This flower came as a surprise. Some people like getting a surprise, some are creative in providing them. I have to confess that I'm not great at either creating or receiving surprises. I like to know in advance what is going to happen; then I'm more in control. Yet, there are occasions when I can readily acknowledge the beauty and joy of being surprised. That has increased in my senior years. There is an interesting book called The God of Surprises in which Gerard W. Hughes shares his thoughts on finding God in unexpected places. The Infancy Narrative in Luke's Gospel is a wonderful illustration of the attribute. God's love for us is an ongoing surprise. How do you feel about surprises?

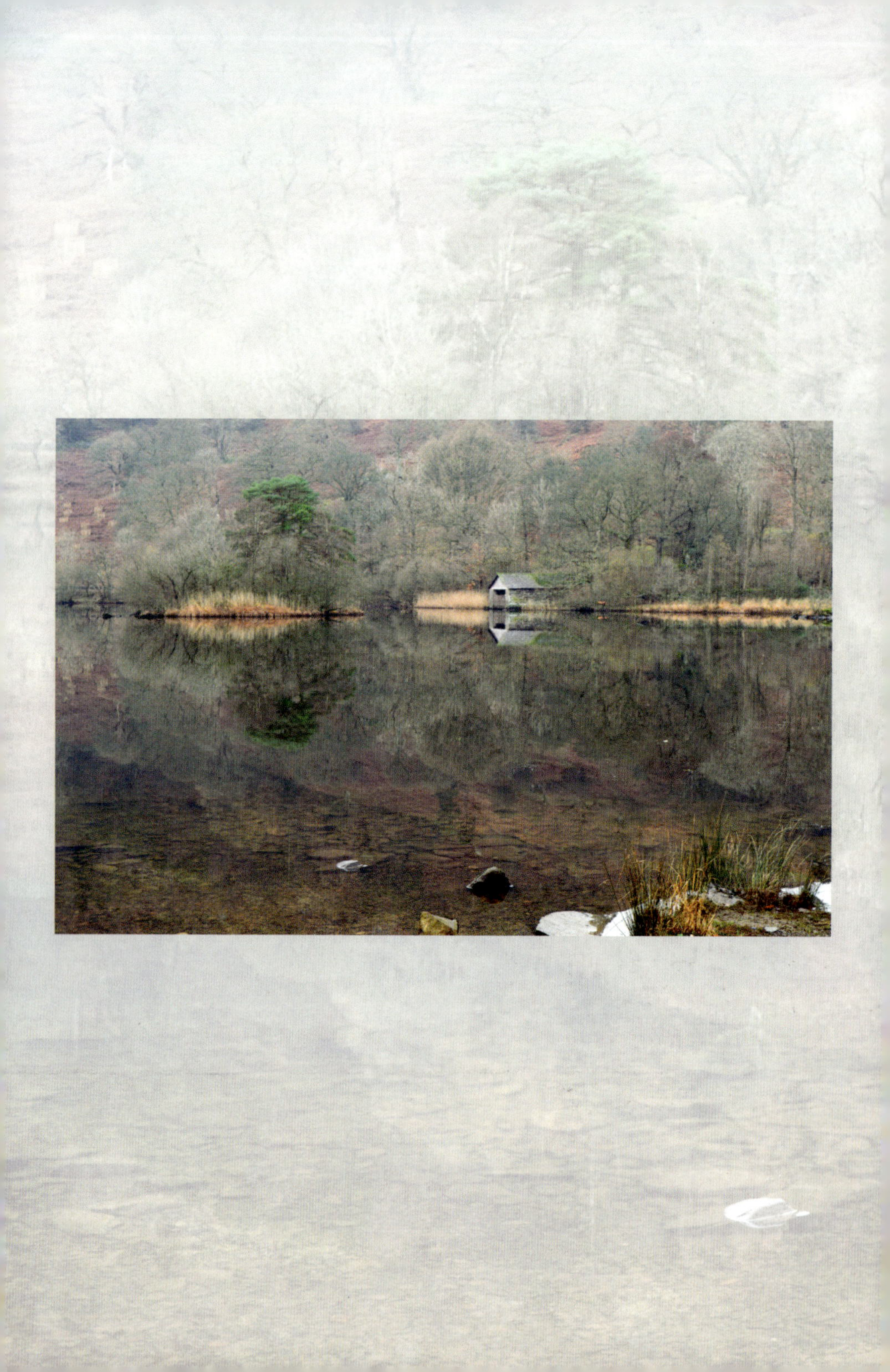

Abundance

I have taken many pictures of this boathouse on Rydal water in the Lake District, perhaps one or two on every visit. This one probably dates back a few years to one of my earliest visits. I'm always fascinated by lakeside boathouses; I can't resist attempting a shot. On this occasion in midwinter, the reflections were stunning, and the gentle contrasts very attractive, with a hint of lingering light mist amidst the trees. I really like the way the russet of the reeds and the one green tree are highlighted, and how in the foreground the green and orange grasses blend harmoniously. The water near the spot from which I took the picture is quite shallow, revealing the underlying stones. The hill in the background rises quite steeply towards the sky.

As we view and ponder a photo like this, there is such a lot to take in. It's like visiting a picture in an art gallery. And, of course, we are unable to hear birdsong, the bark of a dog in the distance, hushed conversations from far off, and we cannot catch the scents lingering in the air. Vision is but one aspect of our amazing human awareness. Abundance! The leaves on a tree, the grains of sand and pebbles on a beach, the stars in the sky, the people in the town, the starling flocks, the fish in the sea… such abundance, and all reflect the abundance of God's love for us. Let's spend some time today absorbing some of the abundance which inundates us.

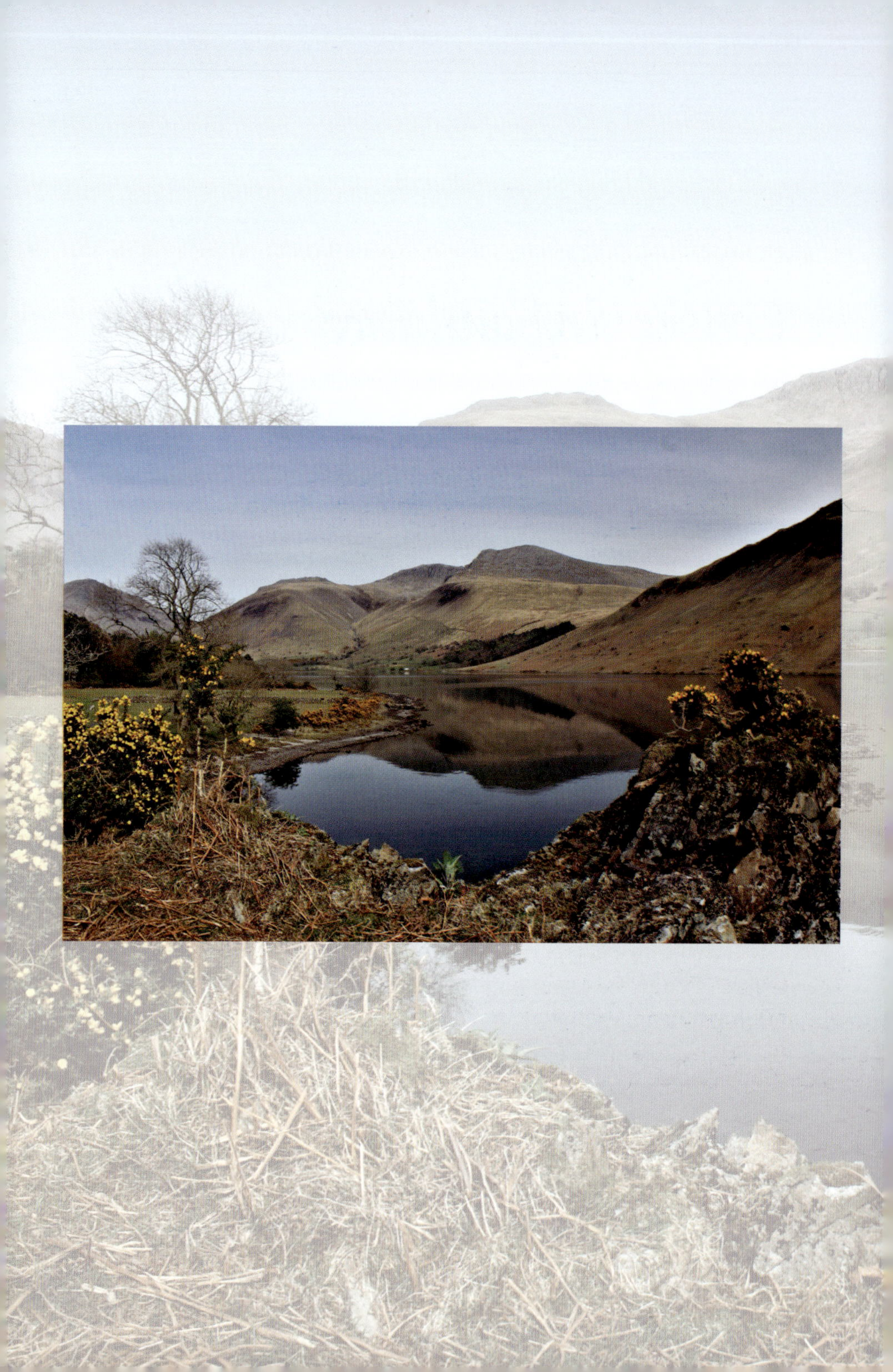

Conserving our Environment

We are in the Lakes again, this time alongside Wastwater, my favourite lake, in early spring. Some years ago, the people of England voted the view of this lake as the finest in the country. The view leads up to Scafell Pike, the highest peak in England. At this time of year, the terrain was struggling to embrace spring; the gorse in flower was the promise of a brighter future, of new life replacing barrenness. This transition occurs each year, a wonderful free gift from nature, not engineered by human beings.

One of the major challenges of our world these days is climate change, with its threat to the environment. Ecological issues have become centre stage. It is our responsibility to be stewards of creation, to preserve the beauty of the countryside and its natural habitats. This is an uncomfortable challenge because it makes demands on the way we are living, but it is a challenge we cannot fail to take up. Let this Wastwater scene stimulate our efforts to become more sensitive, more active, in preserving our heritage for future generations, and saving our world from disaster.

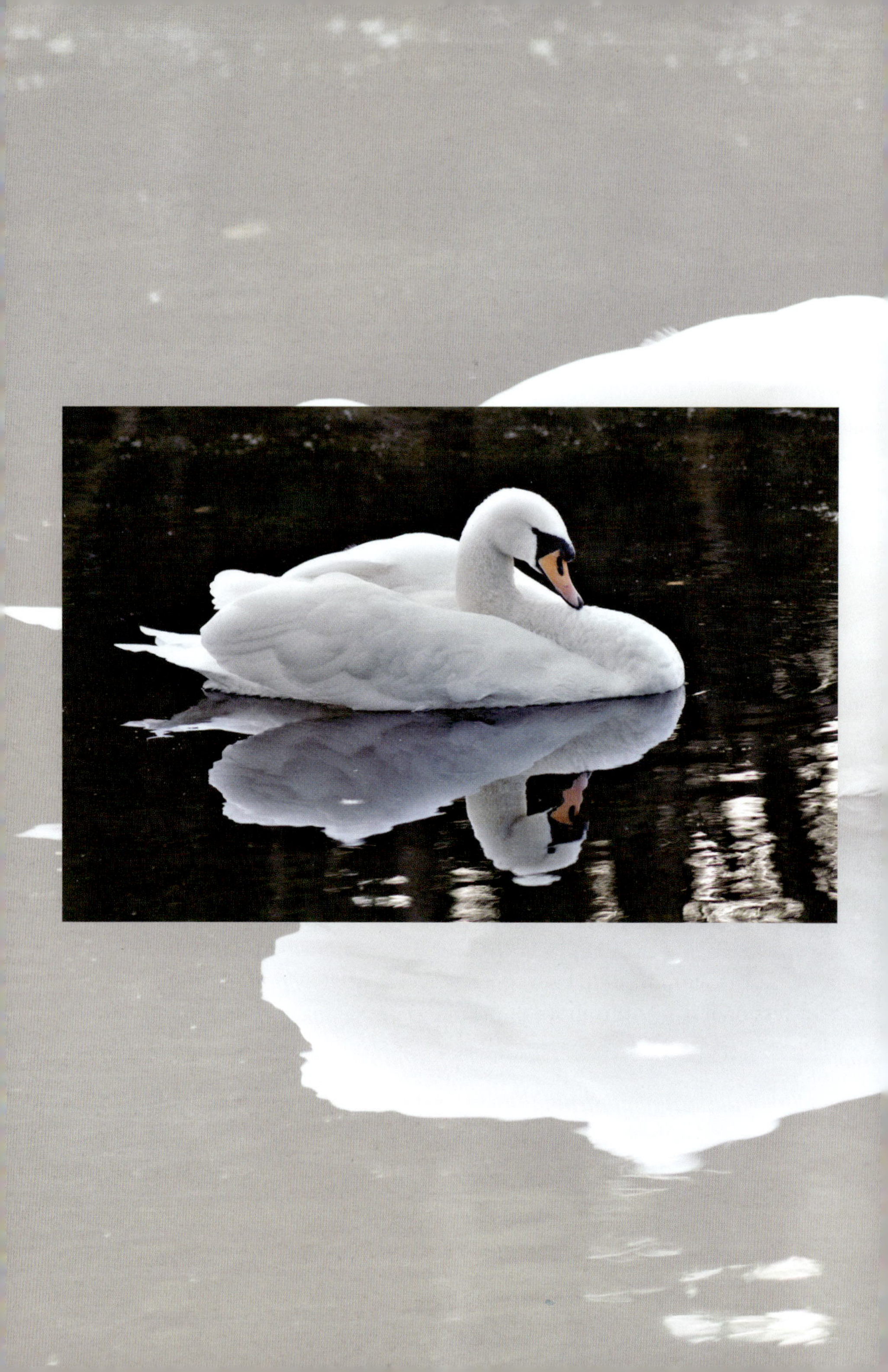

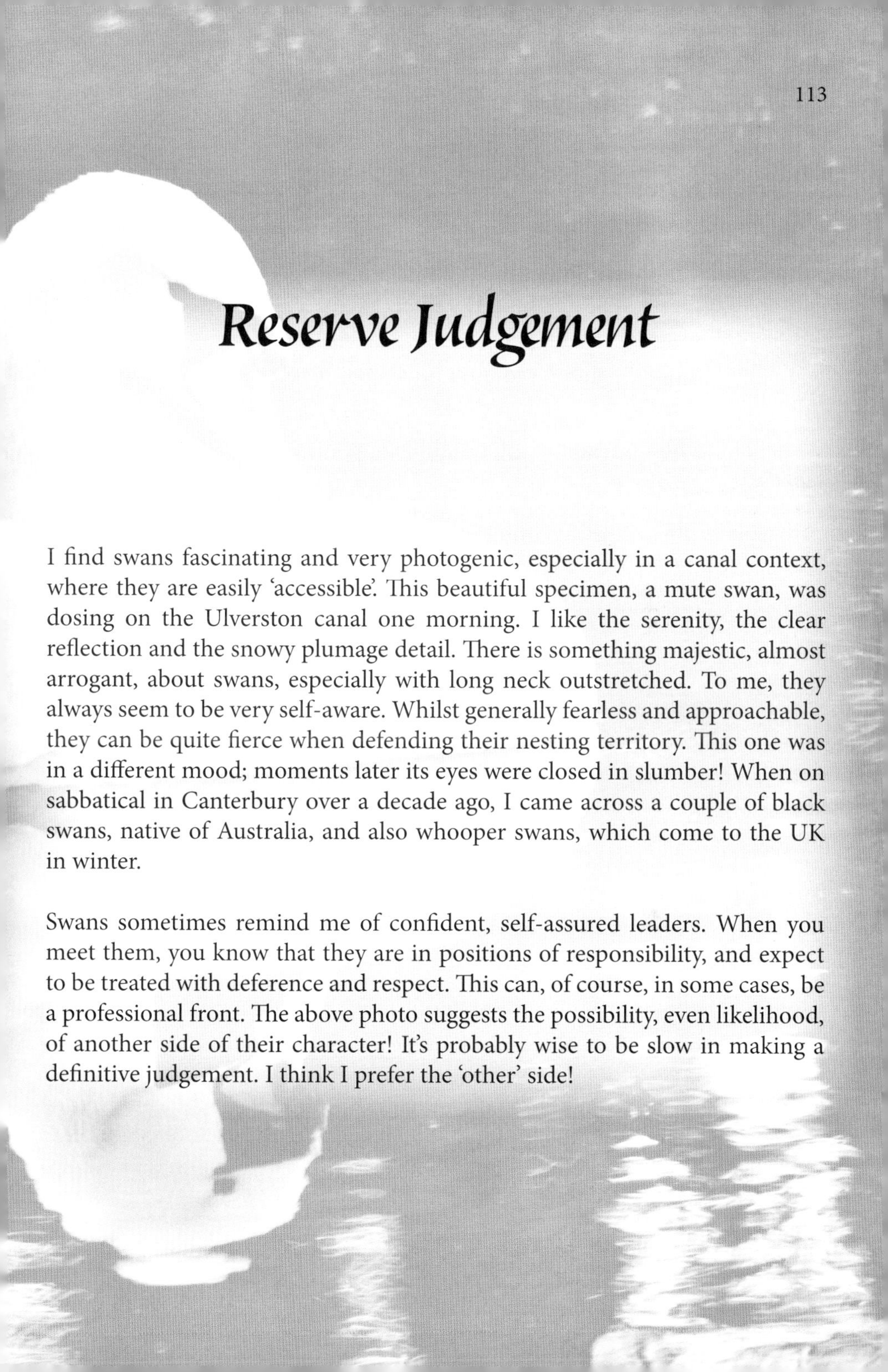

Reserve Judgement

I find swans fascinating and very photogenic, especially in a canal context, where they are easily 'accessible'. This beautiful specimen, a mute swan, was dosing on the Ulverston canal one morning. I like the serenity, the clear reflection and the snowy plumage detail. There is something majestic, almost arrogant, about swans, especially with long neck outstretched. To me, they always seem to be very self-aware. Whilst generally fearless and approachable, they can be quite fierce when defending their nesting territory. This one was in a different mood; moments later its eyes were closed in slumber! When on sabbatical in Canterbury over a decade ago, I came across a couple of black swans, native of Australia, and also whooper swans, which come to the UK in winter.

Swans sometimes remind me of confident, self-assured leaders. When you meet them, you know that they are in positions of responsibility, and expect to be treated with deference and respect. This can, of course, in some cases, be a professional front. The above photo suggests the possibility, even likelihood, of another side of their character! It's probably wise to be slow in making a definitive judgement. I think I prefer the 'other' side!

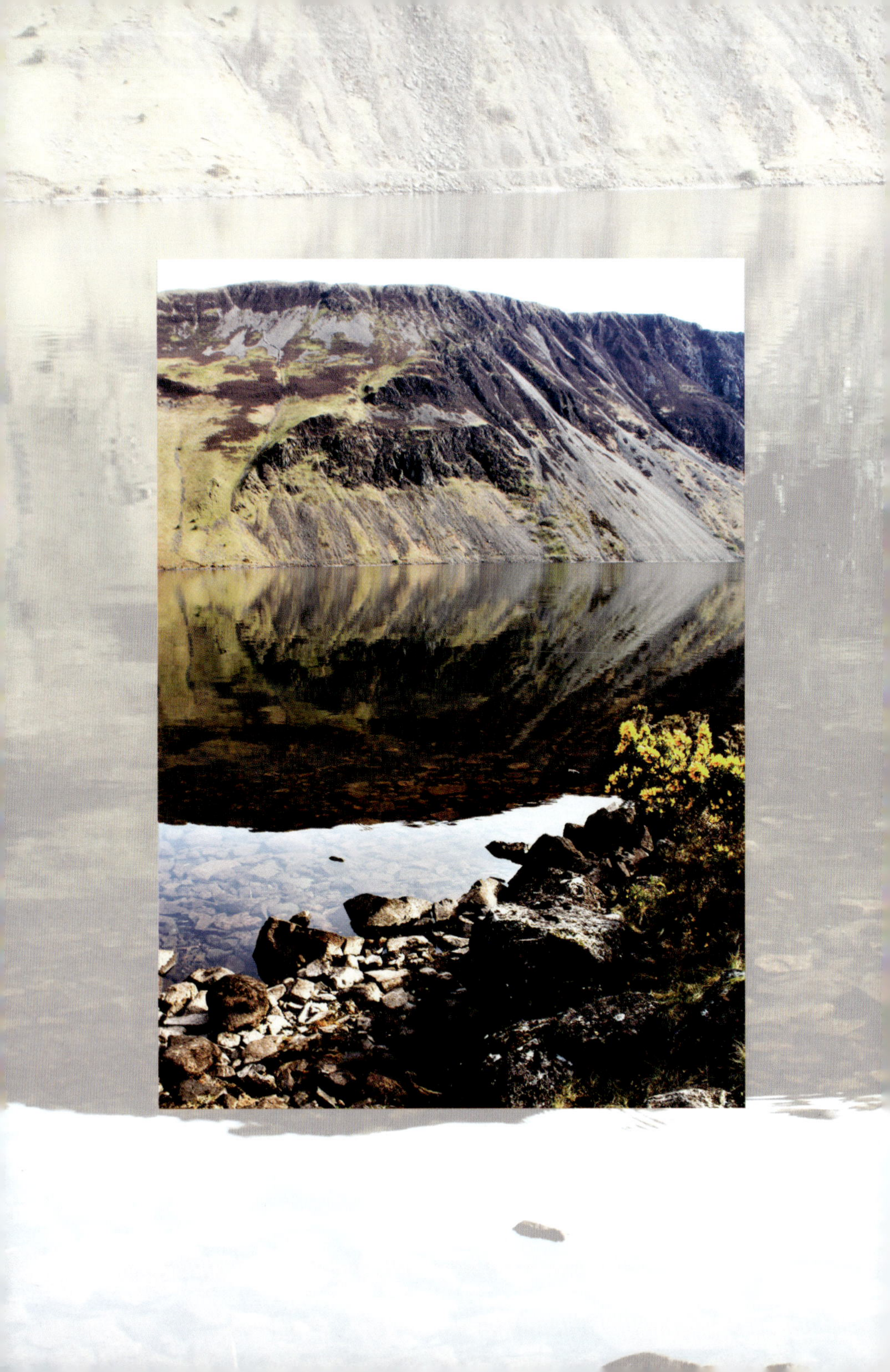

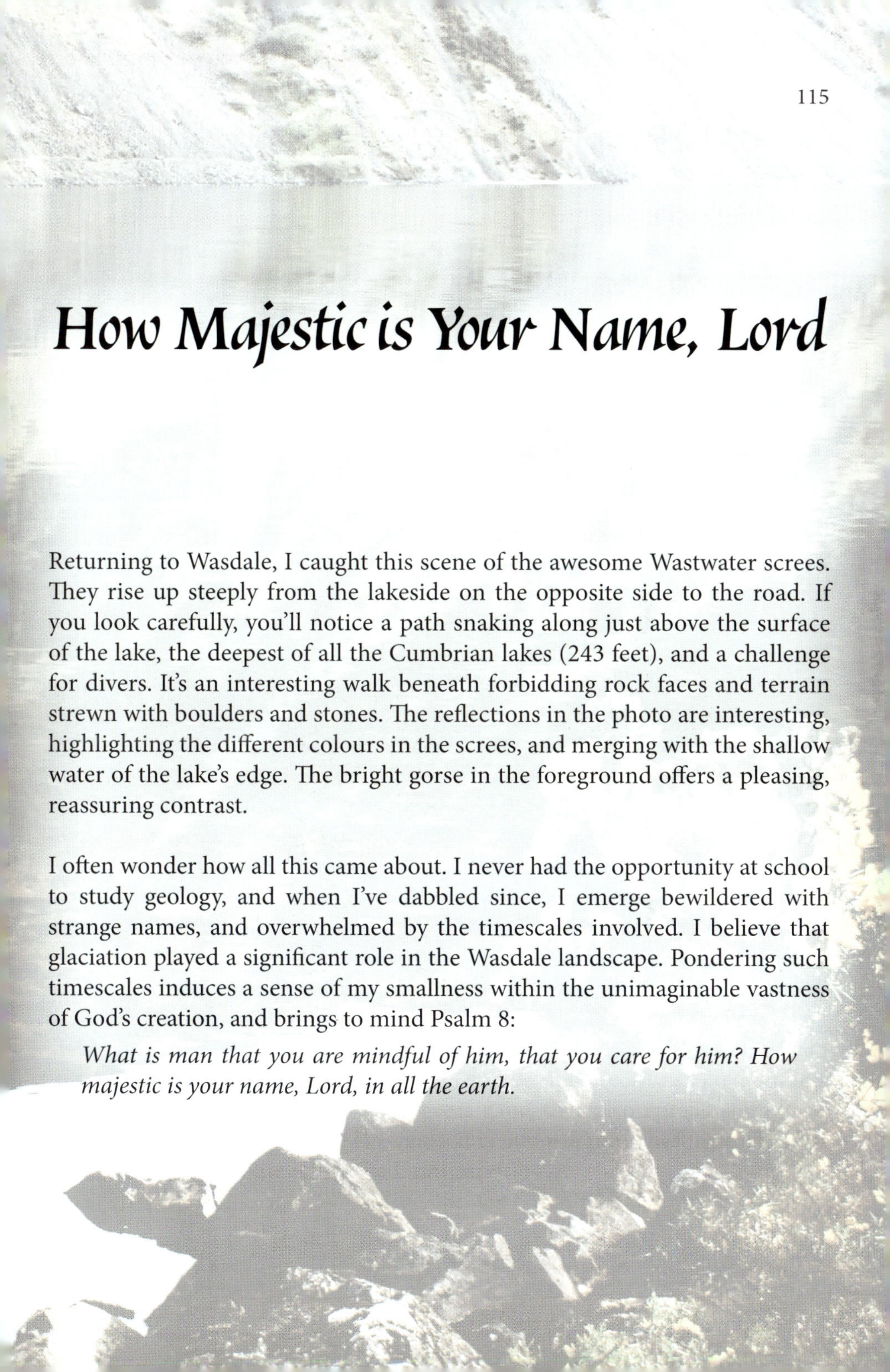

How Majestic is Your Name, Lord

Returning to Wasdale, I caught this scene of the awesome Wastwater screes. They rise up steeply from the lakeside on the opposite side to the road. If you look carefully, you'll notice a path snaking along just above the surface of the lake, the deepest of all the Cumbrian lakes (243 feet), and a challenge for divers. It's an interesting walk beneath forbidding rock faces and terrain strewn with boulders and stones. The reflections in the photo are interesting, highlighting the different colours in the screes, and merging with the shallow water of the lake's edge. The bright gorse in the foreground offers a pleasing, reassuring contrast.

I often wonder how all this came about. I never had the opportunity at school to study geology, and when I've dabbled since, I emerge bewildered with strange names, and overwhelmed by the timescales involved. I believe that glaciation played a significant role in the Wasdale landscape. Pondering such timescales induces a sense of my smallness within the unimaginable vastness of God's creation, and brings to mind Psalm 8:

> *What is man that you are mindful of him, that you care for him? How majestic is your name, Lord, in all the earth.*

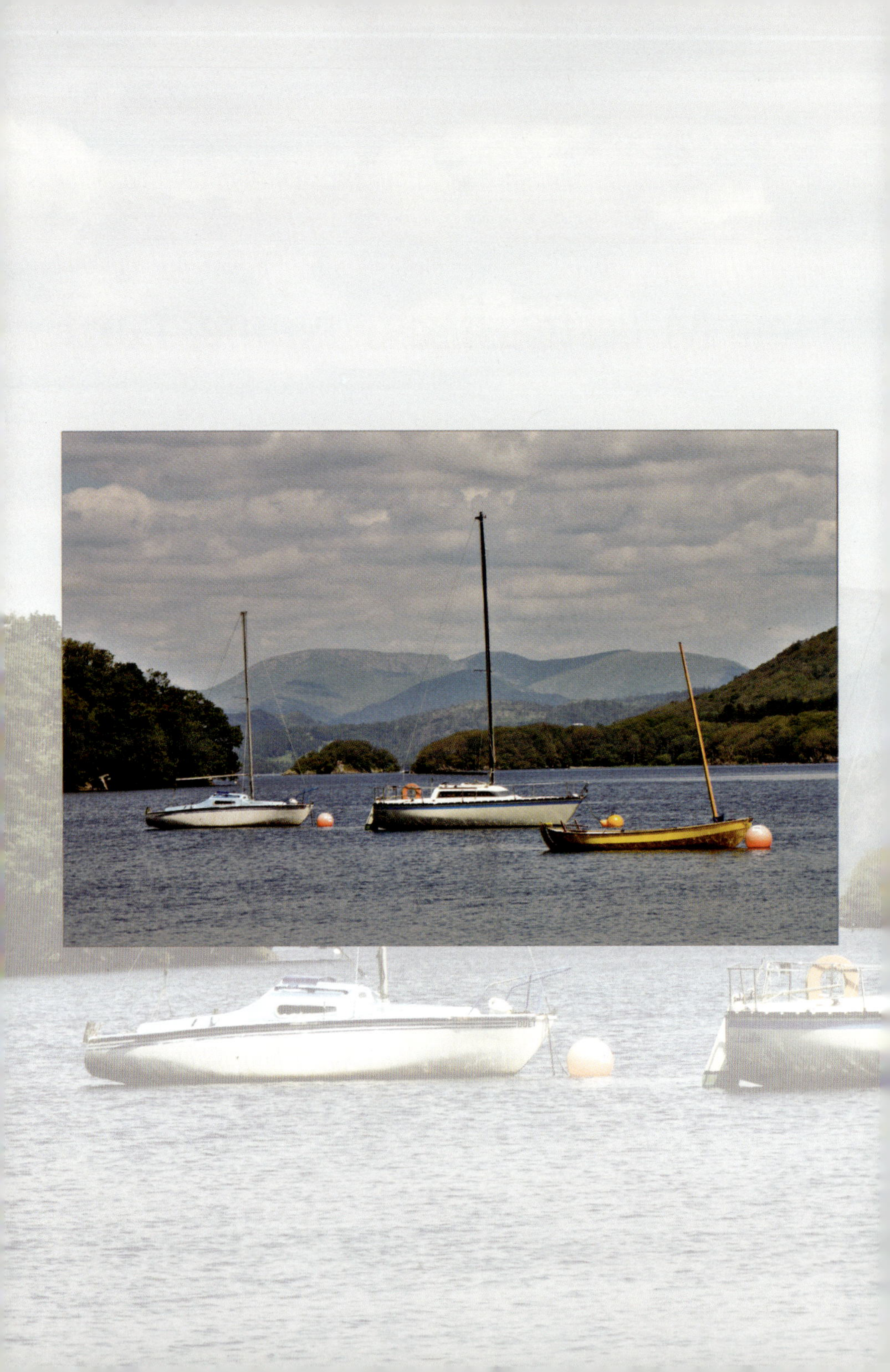

Stillness

I've visited the western side of Lake Coniston often, usually en route for another destination. Recently, prompted by a small roadside carpark near the southern end, I discovered a more secluded spot, and enjoyed exploring the woodland and lakeside. There were several boats moored in the vicinity, including this trio. Unfortunately, there were no reflections, due to too much gentle movement in the water. However, I like the way the lake reflects on the hull of the two right hand boats. The experts say that the human mind and eye prefer odd numbers; three is a favourite. That's true in literature too; even Jesus used a trio in the parable of the compassionate Samaritan. It's interesting how a zoom lens brings the distant hills much closer, and I'm glad one of the yachts isn't white! Yellow, like red, stands out and grabs attention.

The moored yachts, the lack of people on or in the water, the distant, shadowed hills and gentle clouds meld together, and suggest a moment of utter stillness. It's a picture to stop and observe, to allow the peace to embrace you, as if time doesn't matter. It's important to allow that to happen to us. Stillness can powerfully energise.

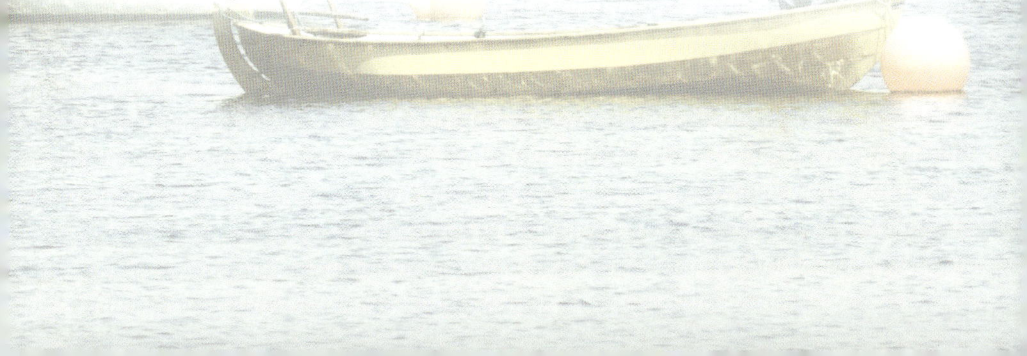

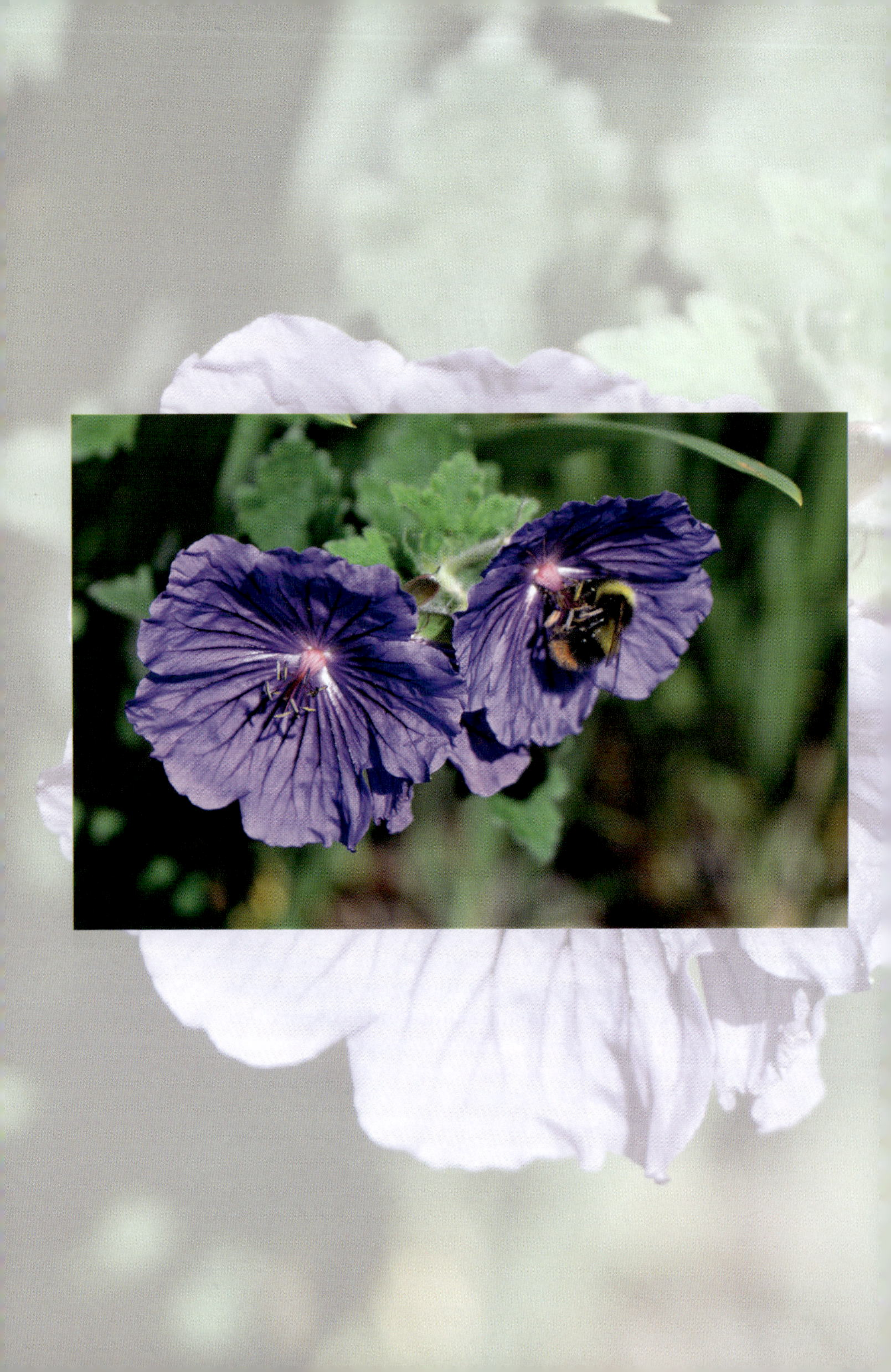

Get Closer

My favourite insect is the bee. Bees are so necessary for the pollination process, and therefore for the beauty of our gardens. They are such busy little creatures. Sadly, there seem to have been far fewer of them in our garden this year. This bee is seeking pollen on a Meadow Cranesbill. These striking flowers with their bluish-lilac hue grow in pairs in clumps, with attractively shaped leaves, a delight in the garden. Somehow, the centre of the flower seems to emanate a burst of light. Getting close, carefully, gently and respectfully, and creating a blurred background, reveals in detail the texture of both flower and bee.

Perhaps there's a lesson there. As human beings in a fast-moving world, with its stress on the 'instant', there is a danger of superficiality, of not really getting 'close in', of missing the depth of things. This can apply to nature in its many forms, to music, literature and art, to fellow humans and to God. Surface living is a tragedy, a wasted opportunity, an invitation to emptiness and poverty of being; so much richness is missed. Getting 'close in', of course, can take time, patience and the odd risk; it demands effort and perseverance, but it can lead to enormous enrichment of mind, heart and soul.

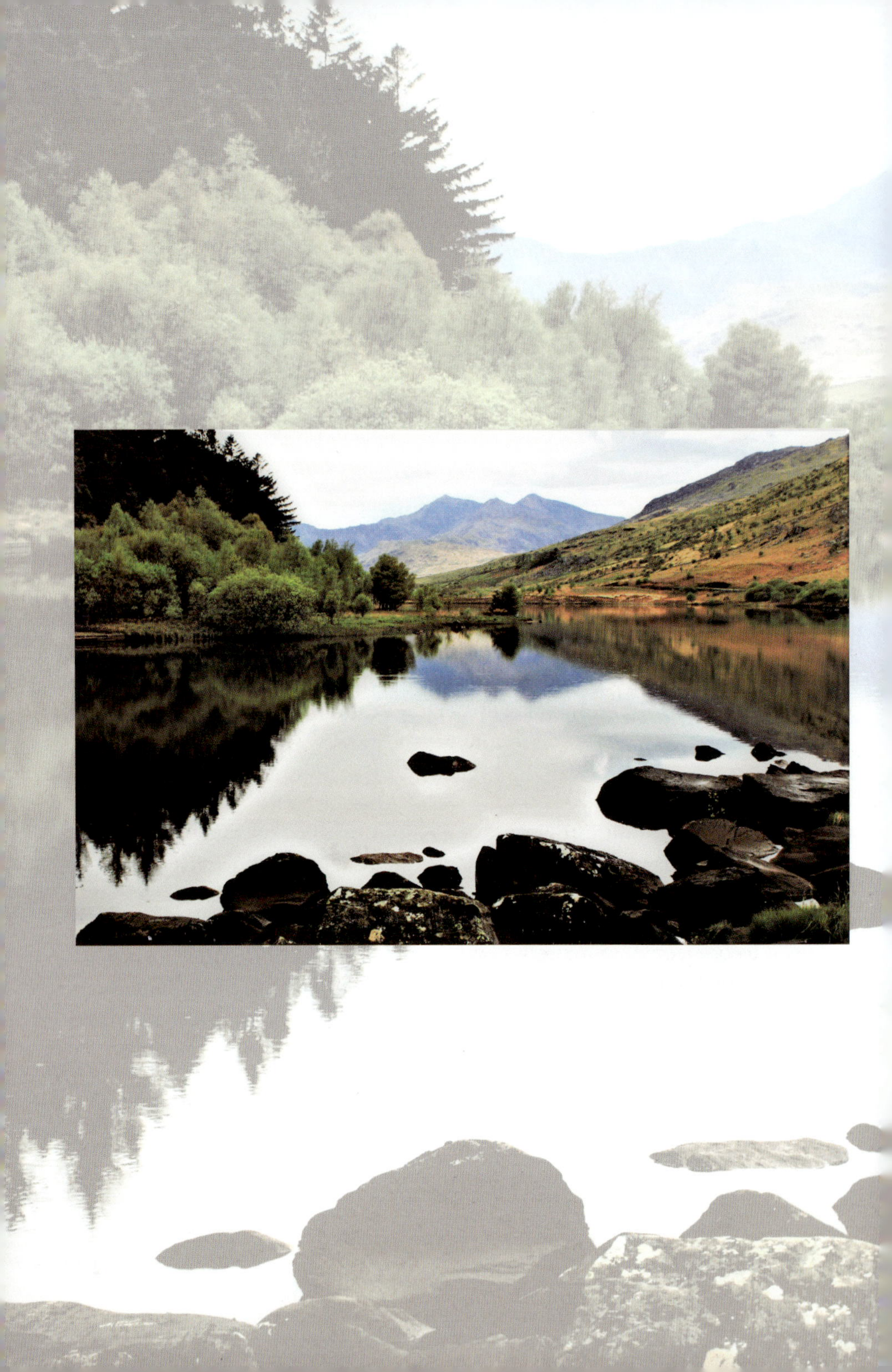

Make the Most of Today

This picture was taken at the head of the twin Llyns (LLynnau Mymbyr) near Capel Curig in Snowdonia (Eryri). As is evident, especially in the blue area of the Llyn, it had started to rain. This spot, some fifty yards from the main road, is a photographer's delight with the interesting rocks in the foreground, the colourful reflections of forest and moorland on either side, and a splendid view of Snowdon in the distance. I've been here a few times to find Snowdon was engulfed in cloud. This day, despite the rain, I was lucky.

One lesson I learnt that day was not to wait for perfect conditions. Often, paradoxically, it is the imperfect conditions which provide the ideal photographic scenario. I'm sure that this is valid for other experiences in life. Often, opportunities are missed because we wait, delay, prevaricate, or because we won't take a risk, and we want the conditions to be perfect before acting. We need to be people who know how to make the most of what is available. Don't miss out today!

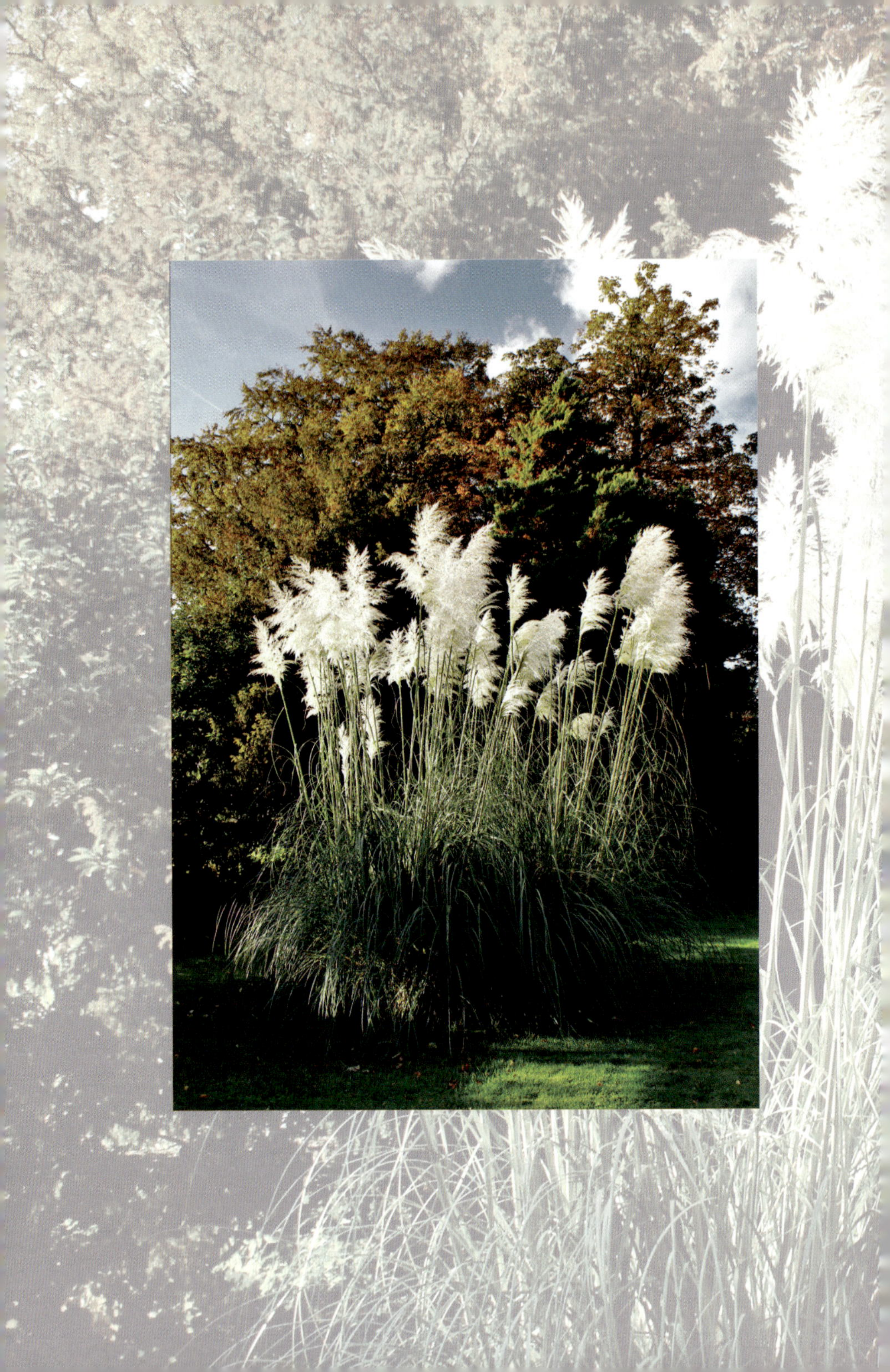

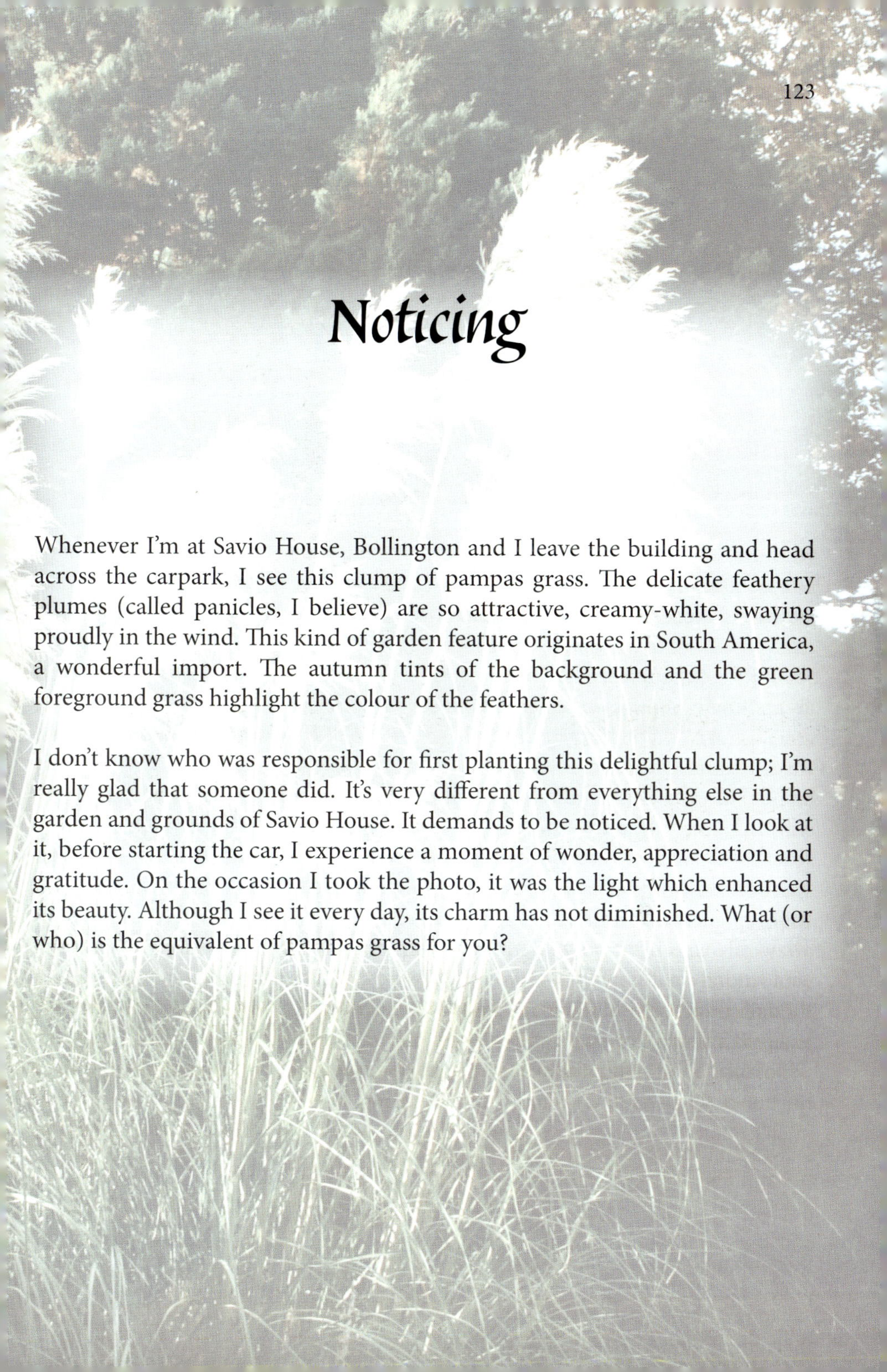

Noticing

Whenever I'm at Savio House, Bollington and I leave the building and head across the carpark, I see this clump of pampas grass. The delicate feathery plumes (called panicles, I believe) are so attractive, creamy-white, swaying proudly in the wind. This kind of garden feature originates in South America, a wonderful import. The autumn tints of the background and the green foreground grass highlight the colour of the feathers.

I don't know who was responsible for first planting this delightful clump; I'm really glad that someone did. It's very different from everything else in the garden and grounds of Savio House. It demands to be noticed. When I look at it, before starting the car, I experience a moment of wonder, appreciation and gratitude. On the occasion I took the photo, it was the light which enhanced its beauty. Although I see it every day, its charm has not diminished. What (or who) is the equivalent of pampas grass for you?

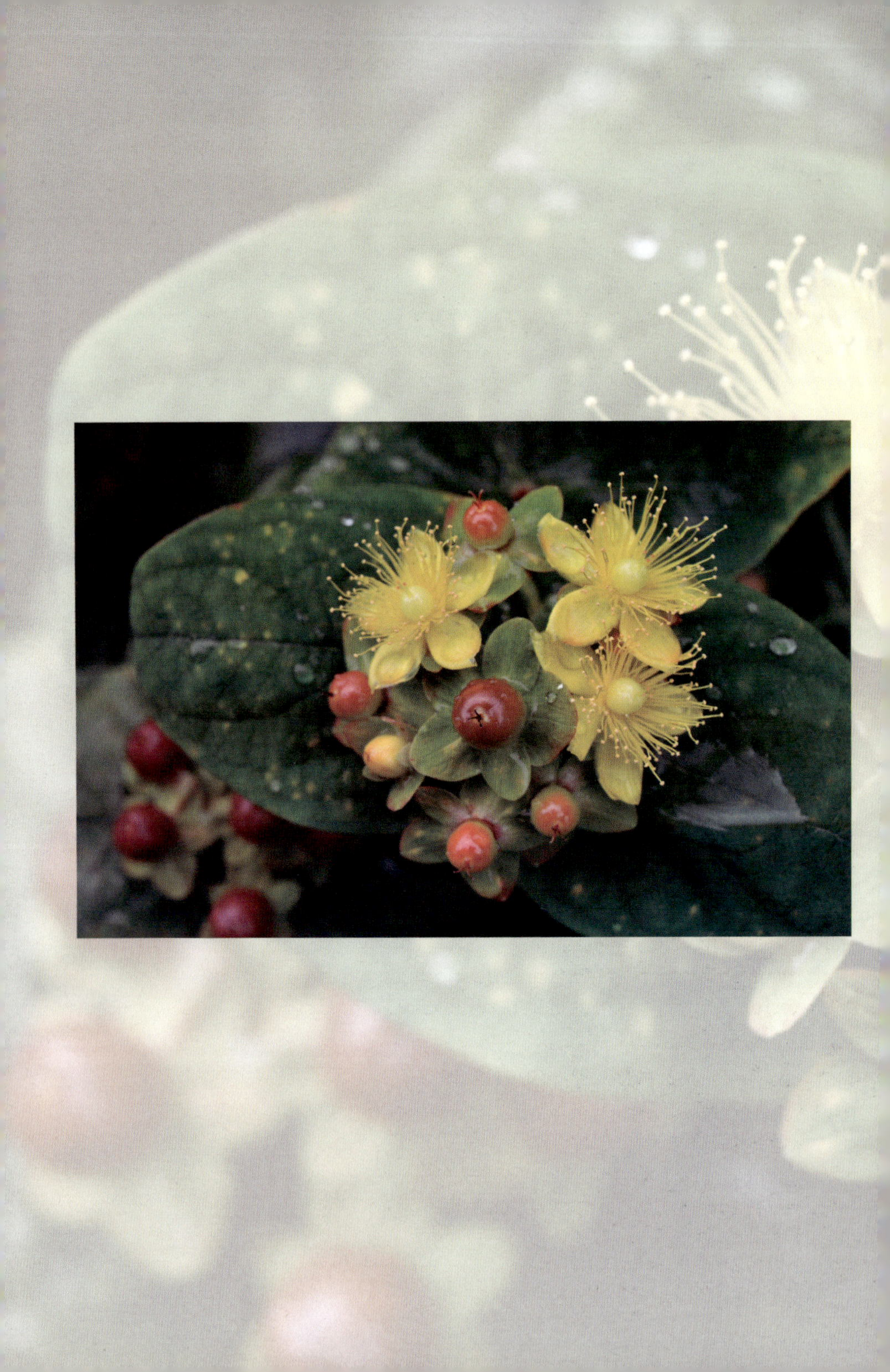

Valuing Differences

One of my favourite flowers is called '*Tutsan*'. I've seen them growing wild and also in gardens. In fact, we have a few of these small shrubs in Thornleigh, where I live. The yellow flowers are eye-catching and very beautiful, standing out from the large green leaves, here showing drops of a recent shower. The orange or red berries are quite bright and shiny; eventually they turn black as the flowers fade. The shrub seems capable of looking after itself, without needing human help. Wonderful!

There's something amazing about the variety in nature, different hues, shapes, textures, ways of surviving and thriving. It's enriching to become aware, and maybe to watch and take notice as the seasons change: the miracle of life. And the same is true for us humans too. At present in the Salesian community where I'm staying, there are twelve of us from ten different countries, with different languages, cultures, life experience and more. There is so much to learn and understand, so much to share and develop. It's so interesting, challenging and wonderful. Let the *tutsan* speak to you today.

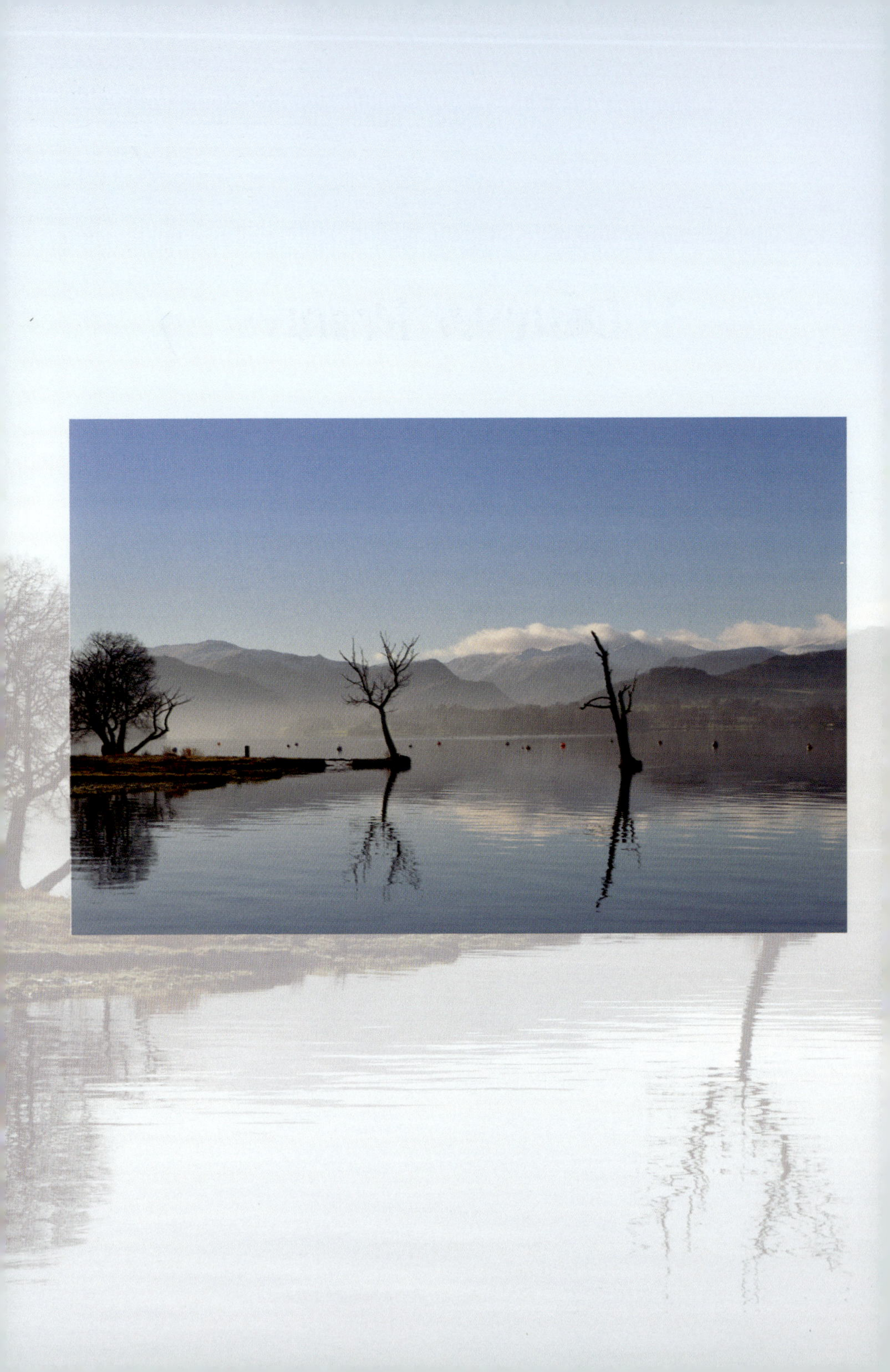

Discover Peace

We finish in Pooley Bridge, beside Ullswater. Instead of a 'lone tree', we have two. It is a late morning in midwinter. The mist is lingering still on the opposite shoreline, and there is snow on the high Helvellyn fells. The trees stand together, cold and bare, almost defiant, amidst the colourful buoys, but instantly claiming our attention with their rippling reflections.

This is a scene of calm and peace: no boats, no people. And such calm and peace is a gift we all crave at times. The external peaceful situation can facilitate inner calm. We need to find time and space to be still in body and mind. It can be so restorative, a source of clarity and new energy. How are you going to find a little peace today?

Other Books by Michael T. Winstanley SDB

Advent Journey, An. Bolton: Don Bosco Publications, 2014.

Alive! The Gospel Resurrection Narratives: Then and Now. Bolton: Don Bosco Publications, 2018.

Come and See. London: Darton, Longman and Todd, 1985.

Don Bosco's Gospel Way. Bolton: Don Bosco Publications, 2002.

Into Your Hands. Homebush, NSW: St Paul's Publications, 1994.

Introduction to John An. Bolton: Don Bosco Publications, 2021.

Introduction to Luke, An. Bolton: Don Bosco Publications, 2022.

Introduction to Mark An. Bolton: Don Bosco Publications, 2021.

Introduction to Matthew, An. Bolton: Don Bosco Publications, 2022.

Jesus and the Little People. Bolton: Don Bosco Publications, 2012.

Jesus and the Young People. Bolton: Don Bosco Publications, 2020.

Lenten Sundays. Bolton: Don Bosco Publications, 2011.

Salesian Gospel Spirituality: An Exploration, Bolton: Don Bosco Publications, 2020.

Scripture, Sacraments, Sprituality. Essex: McCrimmon Publishing Co. Ltd., 2002.

Symbols and Spirituality. Bolton: Don Bosco Publications, 2007.

Walking with Luke: Thematic Studies in the Lukan Narrative with Reflections Bolton: Don Bosco Publications, 2017.